POACHER'S CREED

NO CLOSED SEASON

POACHER'S CREED
NO CLOSED SEASON

By

John Wasserman

ISBN 978-0-578-28619-8

www.johnwasserman.com

The incidents recounted in this book are real; however, the stories are based on my memories over a period of years and may differ from the memories of others. I admit to taking some creative liberties with events and to re-creating some of the dialog. I have also given the poachers and their associates fictitious names and have altered their physical descriptions. Any resemblance to actual persons, living or dead, is entirely coincidental.

DEDICATION

For Bill, my strikingly handsome identical twin brother, who was incredibly helpful in getting my books *Woods Cop*, and *Poacher's Creed* published.

Introduction

Each chapter of this book illustrates an important part of my life during my long career as a state game warden.

Ride with me as I chase notorious poachers, patrol the Yukon Territory of Canada, and prosecute the first DNA game law case in the history of Pennsylvania.

Follow me as I work with US Fish & Wildlife undercover agents who infiltrate one of the largest poaching operations in the history of the United States.

Fly with me to discover why deer carcasses were thrown into the sky from an Army National Guard helicopter while hovering above the Fish Dam Run Wild Area.

Walk with me while you learn about the history of the fisher reintroduction to Pennsylvania.

I begin with a sequel to my first book, *WOODS COP: Thirty-four Years a State Game Warden.* I borrowed a few paragraphs from the ending as a memory refresher for my former readers. The final chapter of that book was about Coyotee Boy, an infamous hardcore poacher who delighted in snitching on his friends. As the story continues in this book, Coyotee Boy makes some very bad life decisions that cause severe consequences for him. I hope you enjoy it!

"To those devoid of imagination, a blank place on the map is a useless waste; to others, the most valuable part."
— Aldo Leopold

DEATH WISH

I watched as Coyotee Boy jumped inside his truck and slammed the door shut. "The game is on!" he cried. "You'll never catch me again, and the deer are gonna drop like flies!" Then he dropped his pickup into gear and sped onto the highway toward Renovo.

I knew Coyotee Boy was serious and that he would be poaching a lot of deer. I was spread thin with a four hundred and fifty square mile patrol district and only one deputy. The odds were clearly in his favor, and he was known for thrill kills—just dropping them where they stood and driving away.

I drove home feeling a bit depressed knowing that even if I caught him poaching again, he'd never quit. I walked inside, sat down at my desk, and thought long and hard about how to stop the impending slaughter of perhaps hundreds of deer.

Coyotee Boy had played me; no doubt about it. I fell for his lies and believed that he had quit poaching after he became my informant. He was a good snitch—so good that I actually *wanted* to believe he'd gone straight. Thanks to Coyotee Boy, I was able to arrest poachers I'd been chasing for years without any luck. But deep inside, I sensed that something wasn't right. Coyotee Boy actually enjoyed being a snitch. He would even ride along with some of his best friends while they poached deer, just so he could set them up for an arrest. And then there was the day he gave me enough information on his brother Wolfe to arrest him too! Coyotee Boy was a cold-blooded snake as far as I was concerned, and a little bit crazy as well. Maybe more than a little bit.

I had to stop using him as a snitch for his own protection. It was getting too dangerous for him because some of the locals were beginning to suspect that he was an informant. But instead of thanking me, he became enraged and told me he was going back to his old ways again: Thrill kills— shooting deer by the dozens and letting them lay.

He knew I'd be looking for him but he didn't care. After working with me as an informant, he became very familiar with the way I worked, where I patrolled, and the areas I watched closely. He wasn't worried about me at all.

But I knew something that *would* worry him. I remembered watching him tremble in fear that day when Big Nasty walked into the courtroom.

I'll never forget it. Coyotee Boy had my witness Joey scared to death as he sat staring at him with cold eyes of intimidation. That's when Joey told me he was feeling sick and that he had to go. He was about to get up and walk out, leaving me without a chance of convicting Coyotee Boy for killing all of those deer.

Then came Big Nasty. He walked into the courtroom, bigger than life. Had to lower his head under the doorway as he stepped inside. He wore jeans and an open collar flannel shirt, showing the tattoo of a rattlesnake coiled around his neck, its head on one side and tail on the other. The mouth was wide open with huge fangs, and the tail was raised with sixteen rattles. His brown hair was neatly trimmed in a Mohawk, four inches wide and one inch high, head shaved to the scalp on each side. The man's cheekbones were pronounced and high, his eyes dark and intense. A razor-like scar flowed across the bridge of his nose and down the left side of his face. His forearms were thick and vascular, almost the same diameter as his huge upper arms. Frank Frazetta's epic painting of Conan the Barbarian came to mind.

Joey stood up to greet him. Now he was at ease as Big Nasty embraced him with his right arm and slapped his back twice with his left hand. Big smiled at me briefly, and then I saw the fire in his eyes as he turned to face Coyotee Boy.

Coyote Boy quickly dropped his head and looked down at the desk in front of him. He tried to hide it, but I could see a slight shiver in his shoulders. Joey had nothing to fear. Big Nasty, without saying a word, had sent an unmistakable message to Coyotee Boy. Nobody wants Big Nasty mad at them. Nobody!

I shook the memory out of my head and reached for the phone and dialed. I hadn't talked to Big Nasty in quite some time, but I knew I could rely on him for help with Coyotee Boy. Big disliked poachers as much as I did, and Coyotee Boy was the most ruthless of them all.

"Hello?" came a gruff and familiar voice on the other end of the phone.

"Hey Big, it's John. I have a favor to ask."

"Anything for you brother, you know that."

"Coyotee Boy is going to be back at it again, killing a lot of deer and leaving them lay. It's personal this time…with him at least."

"How do you know?"

"That's what he told me earlier today."

"I'm not so sure. He's leaving the area, John. He got some kind of high paying construction job out near Scranton."

"Are you sure?"

"Positive. Did you want me to do something to him?"

"No Big. You know better than that. I was thinking about a man-to-man sit-down with him. Just the three of us. But it looks like that won't be necessary now."

Big Nasty was my closest friend. We were both family men, and we were also loners, preferring to avoid the company of others. I had cited him in the past for a technical violation of the Game Law, even served a search warrant on him once. We were two men who should have been at odds with each other, but eventually formed a bond because of our deep interest in the outdoors and mutual disrespect for poachers.

During the off season, I competed as a champion powerlifter, and we would lift weights together. I had to work hard at it while Big was one of those guys who, so it seemed, just had to look at a barbell to gain muscle. He was a true mesomorph, a genetic freak of nature.

His days of being a quick-tempered brawler were long gone, but I don't think anyone knew it except for his family and me. His reputation stayed with him long after he quit drinking and became a loving husband and father with a deep appreciation of nature.

After learning that Coyotee Boy moved away from my patrol district, I was able to work a more relaxed schedule. I had been much more active at night when Coyotee Boy was my informant, and while I would still work some nighttime hours, I planned to spend more time on daylight patrols.

The scent of damp forest leaves mingled with pine needles and the sweet, woody fragrance of ferns was intoxicating. It was a beautiful, warm September afternoon, and after a long day of foot patrol along some steep forested side-hills, I started for home. Sunlight was fading fast, and I looked forward to a hot meal and some rest and relaxation. Years had passed since Coyotee Boy left the area, and I was enjoying my long hikes in the big woods now that he was gone.

But supper would have to wait. As soon as I opened the front door, I saw the red message indicator flashing on the tape recorder by my desk phone. I walked over and pushed the play button.

"Call me, John. He's back."

It was Big Nasty, and I knew he had to be talking about Coyotee Boy. The call was placed early in the morning, shortly after I left the house. I sat down at my desk and stared at the ceiling for a moment, almost wishing I hadn't listened to the message. Then I picked up the handset and dialed. Had to. Something bad happened. I could sense it in Big's voice.

Big answered the phone after the first ring. He told me that he'd been waiting with his daughter at the school bus stop near his home along Young Woman's Creek when he heard a vehicle approaching on the gravel road. As it began to round a curve a short distance away, it came to an abrupt stop. He could only see the front bumper and grille. Suddenly there came a deafening gunshot and immediately afterward the car raced by them with the rear end fishtailing as its tires sprayed gravel everywhere. Big grabbed his daughter and yanked her away from the road. He was able to see a female driving the car, while a man in the passenger seat pointed a rifle barrel out the side window, covering his face with his arm as they raced by. Big told his daughter to run home. There was an old logging trail through the woods that led to their house. She knew it well.

Big's truck was backed into the logging trail. He ran to it, jumped inside, and sped after the car, an older model Chevy Impala, dark blue in color. As he approached the village of North Bend, some six miles away, Big finally saw the taillights of the Chevy. It was approaching Route 120, and Big hoped the car would have to stop at the intersection for oncoming traffic. Route 120, also known as the Bucktail Trail Scenic Highway, was the main route from Lock Haven to Renovo and beyond.

As luck would have it, five tri-axle dump trucks loaded with stone were traveling toward the intersection, and the Chevy had to stop and wait for them to pass by. Big slammed on the brakes, his truck stopping only inches away from the Chevy. He jumped out and ran up to the passenger side of the car with complete disregard for his own personal safety. After all, there was a man with a gun seated there.

The man had his face tucked down with both hands grasping the back of his head so that he wouldn't be recognized. Big grabbed the doorhandle and pulled on it, but it was locked.

"Open the door you coward!" he roared.

15

The female driver let out a scream of panic, her male passenger wouldn't budge. Big slammed a massive fist against the roof and ordered him to get out once again. The last truck was passing by, so in a final attempt to reach the man, Big grabbed the door handle and yanked on it, snapping it clean off the locked door.

The driver stepped on the gas and her passenger turned his head to look at Big as she sped through the intersection and made a sharp left toward Lock Haven. Big recognized him immediately, his fist still clenching the broken door handle as they sped off (it sits on his fireplace mantle to this day). It was Coyotee Boy.

He could have shot you!" I scolded.

"If he shot me, I would have broken more than just the door handle," snorted Big.

Anyone else saying that would have me shaking my head. But somehow it seemed completely normal coming from Big Nasty. He looked like he just stepped out of a Walt Disney cinematic movie script. The invincible villain, bulletproof and ready to rumble.

"Hey Big, think of your family and don't do anything like that again!" I said.

"You're right, brother. I appreciate that."

"Did you get a license number?"

"No, but you'll recognize the car."

"Why?"

"The roof is dented."

"Much?"

"Yeah, I pounded on it pretty hard."

"How's your hand?"

Big shrugged. "It's swelled up a bit."

"So, it must be a big dent, I mean, in order for it to be obvious?"

"Yeah…I might be in trouble for that."

It was near dark, so I told Big I would meet him the following day and we could look for any creature that Coyotee Boy may have shot, wounded, or killed.

We met early the next morning and went to the location where the car had stopped and the shot was fired. A glint of sunlight reflected off of something lying on the edge of the road. It was a brass shell casing from a .308 caliber rifle. I grabbed it, showed it to Big with a big smile on my face, and stuffed it in my pocket.

"This is an important piece of evidence, and it corroborates what you witnessed." I told him.

"Yeah, I get it John. Otherwise, it would just be my word against his with nothing to back it up."

"Exactly."

We examined the surrounding forest for any sign of blood, or perhaps a carcass, but found nothing. While we were searching, Big told me he had some new information about Coyotee Boy. According to the local rumor mill, Coyotee Boy had recently served time in prison for an armed burglary he committed while he was living out by Scranton. I told Big if it was true, that meant he was a convicted felon, and the mere possession of a firearm would be a serious crime. A conviction in court could send him back to prison for several years.

"Big, now do you understand why I was upset with you yesterday? If a man is facing prison, there's no telling what he might do to a law enforcement officer, let alone a civilian. One of our wardens was shot and killed recently after stopping a convicted felon for poaching a deer. The felon got the drop on him and murdered him because he didn't want to go back to prison for possessing a firearm. The situation was similar to what you saw, where the felon had shot a deer while he was sitting in the passenger side of a pickup truck. The game warden was new, just graduated from our training school. He was only thirty-one years old. We caught the man who killed him; he's in prison now on death row."

"I'd do it all over again John!" insisted Big. "He shot his rifle real close to the bus stop where my daughter was waiting for the bus. And the car was driving recklessly, spinning its wheels, and throwing stones. My daughter could have been hurt. I won't stand for that, no way!"

Big was enraged. His jaw tightened and his hands clenched into tight fists while he turned his gaze up toward the sky. At that moment it was as though I didn't exist. Nothing I said mattered. I'd never seen him so angry.

"Big!" I shouted. "Calm down!" But he couldn't hear me, or so it seemed. He just stood there, rock solid, looking up at the clouds as though the world was his.

It was a warm afternoon, and the sleeves of his blue denim shirt were rolled back to his elbows. The veins in his sinewy forearms bulged as though they were about to burst, and his neck seemed to thicken and swell. I'd only seen this in the gym when an elite athlete's muscles were pumped full of blood after an episode of very heavy lifting. Big had been relaxed just seconds ago, and somehow his anger was affecting him physically! I'd never seen anything like it, and I'd been competing in powerlifting for decades. It was downright scary! At that moment I thanked the Lord we were close friends, but I still found myself subconsciously taking a step back.

I thought back to what Joey the bartender told me a few years ago when he finally decided to testify against Coyotee Boy, a man he was deathly afraid of: "I had two bad choices," Joey said. "Did I want Coyotee Boy mad at me, or Big Nasty? The decision was easy. Nobody wants Big Nasty mad at them." I didn't really understand Joey until today, until this moment. He knew Big Nasty well. He was one of Joey's best customers at the bar years ago. Joey must have seen it too.

Suddenly Big Nasty turned his head toward me. "Sorry John, but that just ain't like me anymore. I know you were just concerned for my safety."

Thankfully, Big was starting to relax. The fire in his eyes was subsiding, his neck and forearms seemed normal again, and he was composed.

"No problem Big. I'd have been angry too if it were my daughter." I tried to shake the entire episode off, but what I had experienced was eerie. If we weren't close friends, I would have been looking for an excuse to leave, to get out of the woods and away from him. There was something wild and primitive about the man.

"So, the story is true," I muttered softly to myself without realizing that Big could hear me.

"What story?" Big asked.

"You, climbing up on the bar at a taproom in Williamsport, ripping off your shirt and kicking mugs full of beer onto three bikers. Gang members no less!"

"Well...I was drinking hard that day, and I was angry."

"About what?"

"I don't remember what I was angry about. Back then it seemed like I was always angry, and drinking alcohol just made me angrier. But all of that happened before I quit drinking."

He paused for a moment, and then smiled broadly, "I can't believe they turned their backs and walked out of the taproom. I thought we were gonna fight." Big laughed and shook his head from side to side.

He didn't know. Had no idea! Those bikers must have seen it too.

We spent the next hour looking for a blood trail or the carcass of an animal but found nothing. Coyotee Boy must have missed his target. That was hard for me to believe, but there wasn't anything to indicate an animal had been wounded or killed. Coyotee Boy doesn't miss, I thought to myself. This is a man who has the ability to shoot a deer through the eye at one hundred yards with a .22 caliber rifle. It's his modus operandi, his trademark or brand that I had found on so many deer carcasses over the years.

"Hey Big, I think we should call it off, there's nothing here. I'll check his criminal record when I get home, and if he is a felon, I'll file unlawful firearm possession charges against him."

"Okay John, but before we give up, I know of a camp he may be staying at."

"Where?"

"Up Summerson Mountain."

"That's nearby; let's go over and see if he's there," I said. "But you have to promise to stay inside my vehicle if he's at the camp and let me handle it. Okay?"

"Yep. But if he tries to hurt you…"

"I can handle myself, Big. You know that."

Big nodded that he understood. "No problem, John, I'll stay in the car."

I knew Big meant what he said. He would stay in the car…up to a point. But I was familiar with Coyotee Boy. I'd dealt with him often in the past. I didn't trust him, and I'd never turn my back on him. He could be dangerous, but that's something that comes with the territory. Law enforcement officers accept the constant element of danger, and we deal with it accordingly.

We drove up Summerson Mountain in my patrol vehicle and arrived at the camp mid-day. There wasn't any smoke coming out of the chimney, and there weren't any vehicles parked in the driveway. It was obvious the camp was empty. We got out of my patrol vehicle and walked over to a brick fireplace a few yards away. It still had a few burning embers, and it contained what appeared to be scraps of bone and muscle tissue. A hundred yards from the fireplace, we found the burned carcass of a fawn deer. The deer was only partially skinned and had most of its hide intact. It had been roasted over an open fire in the fireplace after the entrails were removed, and then it was picked apart by whoever was hungry enough to prepare venison in such an abominable fashion.

I photographed the entire scene for evidence, but it would be difficult if not impossible to prove Coyotee Boy had anything to do with this closed season deer kill. Anyone could have done this. The driveway wasn't gated, and camps in the area are often vacant for weeks or months at a time. But in my heart, I knew it was Coyotee Boy.

There wasn't much else we could do, so I took Big back to his truck and headed for home. Then I looked up Coyotee Boy's rap sheet, and sure enough, he had been arrested for a burglary in Scranton. He was convicted of that crime, and for possession of a small amount of cocaine. Coyotee Boy wasn't selling the drug; he was using it himself. This wasn't like the man I had dealt with in the past. Coyotee Boy was a hardcore poacher, but he didn't use drugs. And other than poaching arrests, his record had been clean. Something changed in him after he moved to Scranton, and it wasn't good. A divorce, burglary conviction, drug use, and prison time. Now he was on parole, and if found guilty of possessing a firearm, he was looking at years in the state penitentiary.

The following day I filed a Pennsylvania Crimes Code felony complaint against Coyotee Boy for possessing a firearm as a convicted felon. In addition, I filed the lesser summary offense of possessing a loaded firearm in a motor vehicle under the Pennsylvania Game Law. The Game Law violation was similar in nature to the felony offense, but I believed it was prudent since my primary enforcement authority was under the Game Law.

Coyotee Boy pleaded not guilty to the charges. He was represented by an attorney from the public defender's office, and a jury trial was scheduled for several months later. I expected that a criminal complaint would be filed against Big Nasty for damaging Coyotee Boy's car. However, it didn't happen, and I believed there may have been a tactical reason why. Normally, in a case like this, the suspect would almost certainly file the cross-complaint. It was a serious offense and could be used to pressure the witness to recant his testimony in exchange for a deal to drop all charges against each party.

Two weeks before Coyotee Boy's trial, Big was sitting in his truck while parked at the Bucktail High School near Renovo. He was waiting for his twelve-year-old daughter, Lovely to get out of school so he could take her home. Big's pickup truck was idling, and the radio was blasting *Rough Boy* by the rock band ZZ Top: *I'll shoot it to you straight and look you in the eye. I'm a rough boy, I'm a rough boy. We can make it work; we can make it by. I'm a rough boy, I'm a rough boy...*

Big Nasty was into the music so much that he didn't notice the disheveled figure who was walking up to his truck. Suddenly there came a rapid tapping on the driver's side window: *tap-tap-tap!*

Big whipped his head to the left and rolled down the window. Coyotee Boy was unrecognizable at first glance. His hair was shoulder length and greasy, and he had grown a full beard. His pupils were wide and dilated and he was breathing hard while his entire body seemed to twitch, jerk and tremble simultaneously.

Big Nasty was momentarily stunned, and before he could say a word Coyotee Boy uttered something that could only be explained as a death wish.

"How's that pretty little girl of yours doing?" It was an ill-advised attempt to intimidate the only witness who could lead to his conviction and years of prison time. Then, at that very moment, Big's daughter cried out from the opposite side of his truck. "Daddy, who is that man? I'm scared!"

Big hadn't noticed her standing there and was caught off guard.

In that brief moment, Coyotee Boy was able to turn and run away. Big Nasty jumped out of the truck and chased him, but Coyotee Boy hopped onto his motorcycle and gave it full throttle as Big was only inches away. The rear tire spun and then hooked the asphalt with enough traction for the bike to vault forward, lifting the front tire off the ground, and allowing Coyotee Boy to escape.

Drug use can have a terrible effect on people. It can make them act stupidly, take extraordinary risks, and cause them to say things they will regret.

Big called me later that day to explain what happened. It was obvious to both of us that Coyotee Boy was trying to intimidate Big from testifying against him in court, but there was virtually no chance of proving intimidation of witnesses under the Crimes Code. He hadn't said enough to convince a jury that the comment was an actual threat.

I asked Big to be patient, watch over his daughter, and soon Coyotee Boy would be behind bars. "Proving a charge before a jury can be difficult," I said. "But I think we can get a conviction on the gun possession charge, and he'll spend a few years in prison for that."

"But how can you be sure?" Big asked.

"All I can say is that I'd be very surprised if he gets away with it, so hang in there brother, just two more weeks and it will be over."

"Okay, John. But if I see him again, there may not be any need for a trial."

I knew Big was serious. We were very close...swore an oath of confidence to each other years ago. I know it may seem unusual to some folks, perhaps old-fashioned or a bit odd, but it was an unconditional promise. Afterwards, Big confided some disturbing things to me about his troubled past...dreadful things.

"Don't take this matter into your own hands," I cautioned. "Coyotee Boy will have his day in court. That's how we do things in a civilized world."

"I know, John," said Big. "You're right. I just get so angry sometimes."

Two weeks went by with no sign of Coyotee Boy, and I was beginning to think he wouldn't show up for the trial. Big and I drove to the Clinton County Court of Common Pleas together. Big was wearing a shirt and tie, and although he had shopped for a suit jacket in the small town of Lock

Haven, he wasn't able to find one that would work. A size fifty-four fit his shoulders, but he couldn't get his huge upper arms through the sleeves. His shirt was open at the neck. It was a nice enough shirt, short sleeves with slits up each side in order to fit, white and neatly pressed, but his twenty-inch neck kept the top button from closing. The rattlesnake tattoo on his neck was obvious, and he had the tattoo of a steel-jawed foothold trap on the back of each hand. Both of his forearms were fully "sleeved" with tattoos. I had some concerns about how the jury might perceive him at first, but I was confident he would win them over once he testified. He had a lot of self-confidence, a booming voice, and unwavering eye contact. And he had a great smile, although it was rarely seen.

"Big, make sure you don't lose your temper when you testify," I cautioned. "Coyotee Boy will be across from you seated next to his attorney, and we need to get through this without you exhibiting any hostility toward him. Otherwise, the jury might interpret it as a pre-existing feud between you two, and that would hurt us. We need to get him convicted and back in prison."

"Okay John, I'm willing to try. But I sure hope it works...especially for his sake."

"Stop thinking like that and let the DA do his job" I said. "Now let's get moving. The district attorney is waiting for us. He wants to review everything before presenting the case to the jury."

As we sat at a table across from the district attorney in a conference room, he explained that Big would be called to testify first, and then I would testify about finding the .308 shell casing lying on the roadway. Unfortunately, the district attorney wasn't confident about our chances of getting a conviction. He started to ramble on about how it all boiled down to a solid identification of Coyotee Boy and convincing the jury he wasn't misidentified.

"Misidentified by who?" Big interrupted.

24

"Well, you're the only witness," the district attorney said with a smirk.

Big slowly stood, his thighs brushing across the edge of the table as he rose, causing it to tip toward the attorney's stomach. The lawyer's eyes opened wide as he leaned back on his chair and turned his head toward me, hoping I would take control of the situation. I stared back at him in silence while I tapped Big's ankle with the tip of my shoe, signaling him to back off. Big looked at me, and then back at the district attorney. He paused for a moment and smiled.

"I get it," he said to him. "You were testing me, preparing me for a smart remark that the defense attorney might make during cross examination."

The district attorney pulled a handkerchief from his shirt pocket and dabbed a bead of sweat from each temple. His expression relaxed as his gaze shifted away from me and back to Big.

"Yes, exactly, and you handled it well," he said in an obvious attempt to disguise his uneasiness.

It seemed like Big had become a loose cannon lately, ready to explode. This wasn't like him. Or perhaps one could say it was like him, from back in the days when he was drinking heavily, long before we became friends. Coyotee Boy's veiled threat against Big's daughter had struck a nerve. A fuse had been lit, and I couldn't predict whether or not he'd stay calm during the trial.

The district attorney walked out of the conference room and across the hall to the main courtroom. I explained to Big that he was required to remain alone in the conference room until he was called as a witness. First the jury would be seated, then opening statements would be made by the defense attorney, and the district attorney. Immediately afterwards a deputy sheriff would escort him to the witness stand. I told him the president judge of the Court of Common Pleas would be presiding over the case.

I walked across the hallway to the main courtroom and sat down next to the district attorney. He gave me a sideward glance and muttered something under his breath that I couldn't understand.

"What was that?" I whispered.

"You better get that guy under control!"

"He is under control, sir. I spoke to him a moment ago. Told him to relax."

"About the same amount of control as a junkyard dog, from what I've seen," he shot back.

He was about to say something else, but at that moment the jury was led into the courtroom and seated in a row of chairs to our left. Coyotee Boy and his attorney were seated to our right. And then the judge entered the courtroom. Everyone except for the jury members stood up from their seats and waited for the command to be seated by the bailiff. Then each attorney had a few minutes to address the jury with their opening statements. Immediately afterward, the bailiff called for Big Nasty, and he was escorted into the courtroom by a deputy sheriff. Big walked over to the witness chair beside the judge's bench (a raised wooden podium directly in front of us) and sat down.

I could hear several of the jurors whispering. They were supposed to remain silent, but I believe they were startled by his presence. The man commanded attention whenever he entered a room.

After Big was sworn in by the bailiff, the district attorney asked him to explain to the jury what he had witnessed at the bus stop. Big was composed and relaxed as he testified about what happened that day. The district attorney stopped him just as Big was about to tell the jury about snapping the door handle off Coyotee Boy's car and caving in the roof with his fist. It wasn't relevant. All we needed was a positive identification of Coyotee Boy, and Big had done that. The defense attorney could bring it up during cross examination if he was even aware of it.

We expected the defense attorney to question Big since he was an eyewitness to the violation, and we were surprised when he didn't bother to cross examine him. Big was excused by the judge and allowed to remain in the courtroom.

I was called to the witness stand next. I testified under oath about finding the .308 caliber shell casing on the side of the roadway the following day. I didn't volunteer any information about searching the area near the bus stop for blood or a carcass. Again, it was up to the defense attorney to cross examine me and ask those questions. But he didn't, and I started feeling uneasy about how this was going to end.

At this point, I was convinced that the defense attorney had been duped by Coyotee Boy and his girlfriend, and I was certain they were going to lie under oath about the entire event.

However, it was worse than anything I could have imagined.

Coyotee Boy didn't testify at all. His girlfriend, mother, and brother testified that Coyotee Boy wasn't in the car with them that day. Each swore under oath they were the only people in the car, and that no one fired a shot from a rifle. According to their testimony, there was no rifle, no chase, no Big Nasty.

Now it all made sense to me. I understood why there wasn't any testimony about Big ripping off the door handle and caving in the roof of the car. They wanted the jury to believe none of that happened. That Big never chased after them, which meant he couldn't have positively identified Coyotee Boy. It was their word against his, and Big was outnumbered.

I glanced over at Big, and he was taking all of it in without exhibiting any anger. He must have expected it. After all, Coyotee Boy was well known as a scoundrel and a liar, besides being a poacher. So, I guess it was no surprise to him that Coyotee Boy would have his girlfriend and his family perjure themselves. Their stories were well rehearsed, and it all came down to three against one. Coyotee Boy remained confident while leaning back in his chair, with a cocky grin on his face.

Now it was time for the jury to exit the courtroom and decide Coyotee Boy's fate. We were excused from the courtroom by the judge, and I walked with Big across the hallway to the conference room. Big sat down and lowered his head. I knew he was upset with the way things played out.

"Big, are you okay?"

"Did you see him grinning? NO! I'm not okay!"

"Try to relax," I said. "Let's see what the jury decides and then we can talk."

"Okay John, don't worry, I'm not going to do anything stupid. I have a lot of respect for the judicial system, and for everything you've done for me."

We sat there in silence, waiting to be called back into the courtroom for the verdict. There wasn't anything I could say or do to make Big feel better. We both had a pretty good idea what was coming.

Thirty minutes went by before we were notified that the jury had reached a decision. We walked back into the courtroom and sat down. Soon the bailiff announced, "Please rise," and moments later the judge entered and sat at his bench. Next the jury was escorted into the courtroom and seated. The judge asked if they had reached a verdict. The jury foreman stood up from his chair.

"Yes, Your Honor. We find the defendant not guilty."

I glanced over at Big. He was staring at me. Nothing needed to be said. I could see the fire in his eyes, and I could feel what he was thinking. It was eerie. The only other person in my life where I experienced this was with my identical twin brother, Bill.

After the jury was excused, it was time for the judge to rule on the summary Game Law charge of unlawfully possessing a loaded firearm in a motor vehicle. Summary violations are lesser offenses, and not subjected to decisions by a jury. I knew this but forgot to explain it to Big.

Big was anxious to leave the courtroom, and he didn't understand why we hadn't been excused by the judge. After all it was over...or wasn't it?

The judge looked down from the bench at Coyotee Boy and loudly pronounced that the court found him guilty of the Game Law offense of possessing a loaded firearm in a motor vehicle. It was a vindication of sorts. The jury bought the story told by Coyotee Boy's family, but the judge would have no part of it. I was glad that the judge believed Big Nasty was a credible witness; however, I knew his verdict wouldn't send Coyotee Boy back to prison. And so did Coyotee Boy. The guilty verdict on the Game Law violation only amounted to a fine of several hundred dollars, and a brief hunting and trapping license revocation. It had absolutely no bearing on the more serious felony charge that the jury ruled on moments ago.

Coyotee Boy wasn't going to spend any time in prison.

The judge excused everyone from the courtroom after his verdict. Coyotee Boy was grinning ear to ear as he walked by Big Nasty. Big didn't look at him, but I knew what he was thinking. I could feel it, and it wasn't good.

Many years ago, Big told me he didn't give warnings to people who tried to hurt him. "It's stupid to do that," he grumbled. "If you're serious about stopping a threat, you don't give advance notice. Warnings are just a bluff."

I thanked the district attorney, stood up, and walked over to where Big was sitting. He looked up at me, his face a mixture of bewilderment and despair. "What just happened John?" he asked. "He's not guilty, but he's guilty?"

"Come on Big, let's get out of here and I'll explain everything on the way home."

It was an hour's drive to Big's home, and I was surprised how silent he was. I had explained everything to him, and I could sense that his emotions were churning inside. This wasn't like him at all. Normally, Big wouldn't hold anything back from me. When we were together, he would wear his emotions on his sleeve, tell me anything that was on his mind. Now he just sat there, brooding in silence.

Suddenly his right fist struck slammed into the roof of my state vehicle!

BAM! The echo was deafening. I whipped my head to the right and saw that the roof was dented upward. *How am I going to explain this to my supervisor?* I thought.

"Calm down, Big!" I snapped at him.

"I'm sorry John; I couldn't help it. I'm just so darn angry!"

"Listen to me Big, don't do anything crazy. It's not worth it."

Big didn't say a word. He just sat there, rubbing his fist with his left hand. It was another 30 minutes of complete silence until I pulled into his driveway and shut the motor off.

"You okay?" I asked.

"I'm fine," Big said, but I knew he wasn't.

In an effort to console him, I said, "Remember, the judge believed you, and he is a man who's witnessed thousands of lies in the courtroom during his long career."

"Thanks for that John. And don't worry about the roof, I'll fix it for you."

As I drove home, I was relieved that I wouldn't need to report the roof damage to my supervisor. Any damage to a state issued vehicle was a hassle. There was a lot of paperwork, and the state police had to investigate and sign off on it. Because the damage wasn't due to any negligence on my part, I was eager to take him up on his offer. Big Nasty had worked at an automobile body shop years ago. He could make any dent on a vehicle disappear—make it look like it never happened.

Three weeks later, Lovely stepped off of the school bus near her home. It was a short walk through the woods to the house, something she would do any time her father didn't have the opportunity to walk with her or drive her home in his truck.

When she was halfway to her house, she saw someone standing just off the trail dressed in camouflage and holding a shotgun. It was hunting season, so at first, she wasn't alarmed, although it was unusual to see anyone near that trail. Nobody hunted near Big Nasty's house, even though he didn't own the land. It was state forest, public land, but most people knew this was where Big Nasty hunted and avoided the area.

As Lovely got closer, she realized it was the same person her father had chased away from the school parking lot several months ago. Alarmed, she veered away from the trail and started walking fast. When Lovely was directly across from the hunter, he smiled at her with blackened teeth, and she started to run. He looked like a crazy man, his hair long and tangled in knots, eyes dark and sunk back into his head. She had learned about drug addiction in school, and believed he was seriously addicted. Lovely kept running, faster and faster, home was only a few hundred yards away.

"You're a pretty little girl!" the man shouted. "You'll belong to me some day!" Then he uttered a long howl that rose and fell in pitch, interrupted by a chorus of yips, yaps, and barks. His imitation of a Coyote seemed eerily inhuman.

Lovely dropped the schoolbooks she was carrying and ran for her life, crying, scared to death. Soon she could see her house. She turned her head to look back and tripped over the exposed root of an old white pine. Lovely hit the ground hard, face first. She quickly got up, blood was running from her nose, it was becoming difficult to breathe, but she kept running. Finally, she reached her house, dashed up the porch steps and ran inside. No one was home! It was Friday, and her mother would shop for groceries every Friday afternoon. And Big was working a construction job; he wouldn't be home for another hour.

She was alone.

Lovely grabbed the double-barreled twelve-gauge shotgun leaning beside the front door. She pressed her thumb against a lever that allowed the stock to drop, exposing the chamber. Two rounds of buckshot. Fully loaded! She snapped the stock upward, locking it into place. The shotgun was ready for action, and so was she. Big Nasty had trained her well.

Lovely sat on the floor across from the front door and waited. She was terrified.

Coyotee Boy knew better than to enter the house. His judgment was impaired from drug addiction, but not to the degree that he would dare expose himself to whomever may be home with Lovely. And even if she was alone, he suspected that the home would be like a fortress.

Coyotee Boy's motorcycle was hidden nearby. He picked it up off the forest floor, straddled the seat with his shotgun slung over his shoulder, and sped away at full throttle. Lovely could hear the motorcycle as it raced away from her home. She knew it had to be the man in the woods. Still afraid, she sat trembling and crying until Big Nasty came home from work. Daddy hugged her tightly and told her there was nothing to fear, the bad man would never come back.

The following morning my deputy, Ranger called me on the telephone.

"Hey John, did you hear about Coyotee Boy?"

"No, what happened?"

"His girlfriend reported him as a missing person. He never came home last night, and his motorcycle was found near Baker's Run just off of Route 120. The rear fender was crushed, and it was found just off the shoulder and partially concealed in some brush."

I thanked Ranger for the information and hung up the phone. My first thought was to call Big Nasty. But it was Saturday, and I knew he would be on a day off, so I decided to patrol out by his place and drop by to tell him the news. I put my uniform on, strapped on my Smith & Wesson .357 magnum revolver, and headed out for the big woods along Young Woman's Creek.

As I drove up Big's gravel driveway toward his home, I saw him kneeling in front of his pickup truck. He could hear the stones crunching under the weight of my patrol car and quickly stood to turn in my direction.

I stepped out of my patrol vehicle and walked across the yard toward Big. I kept glancing back toward his house. At any moment, I expected Lovely to open the door and run over to me for a big hug. She always gave me a big hug. Instead, Big just stood there staring at me. I knew something was wrong. I could see it, feel it.

"Hey Big, what's going on, where's Lovely?" I asked.

Big explained in detail what happened the day before. He told me Lovely wouldn't leave the house. She was terrified and having horrible nightmares.

"I'm really sorry to hear about this," I told him. "Coyotee Boy needs to be reckoned with."

Big just nodded his head. That wasn't like him, he was too calm. Then I told Big about the phone call from Ranger earlier in the morning.

"Good riddance," He muttered absently. Again, I thought it odd that he seemed so calm about the news, almost distracted.

"Well, we don't know that he's gone." I said. "It's not like we found a body lying by his motorcycle."

"Yeah John, I guess we don't know what happened to him," said Big. "Hey, I really appreciate you stopping by to tell me about this, but I'm kind of busy right now brother."

He's dismissing me, I thought. *That's not like him at all.*

"What happened to your truck?" I asked as I eyed the right front fender.

"I hit a deer last night and it left a pretty big dent."

I could see the fire in his eyes as he spoke; he seemed to look right through me.

"So…do you want me to write out a permit to possess the meat?"

"Uh…No. It was beat up pretty bad, so I threw it in the river. River's up; it's long gone by now."

I felt uneasy about the way Big was acting. He never lied to me, but it didn't make sense that he'd throw a deer into the river without first taking some of the meat.

Maybe it wasn't a deer he threw into the river, I thought. *Maybe I should...*

Suddenly the front door of the house flew open and Lovely came running over to me and hugged me as hard as she could. I looked over at Big and he smiled warmly.

"Thank you for being Daddy's friend," she said to me. "We love you."

And then she went over to Big, hugged him, and said she loved him too. I don't think I'd ever seen Big appear happier than at that very moment.

Of course, it was a deer. Had to be...

The thin mask of civilization is delicate and easily cast aside. What lies behind is savage and unforgiving.

CHASING BEARS

My patrol truck crawled to the top of an eroded strip mine spoil pile and continued a short distance to the precipice. From here I had a broad view of the surrounding terrain, which had been abandoned decades ago by a surface mining company. The land below had first been timbered, and then the overlying soil and rock was removed, or stripped away. The practice is commonly known as strip mining, and this area had been excavated for coal during a time when mining was largely unregulated. Now all that remained was a lunar-like landscape composed of shale, fragmented sandstone, and various other rock-like residues from eons ago. All of the terrain was highly acidic and hostile to most species of natural vegetation.

It was a chilly, damp November afternoon on the third and final day of the bear season. Tomorrow would be the Thanksgiving Day holiday, and most hunters had packed up and headed for home. I rolled down the windows on both sides of my truck so I could listen for any approaching vehicles, but all I could hear was the wind. It was a dead calm, something one could only experience in the most remote places in northcentral Pennsylvania.

Daylight was beginning to fade, so I decided to get out of the truck for some foot patrol before nightfall. I had only taken a few steps when I noticed something peculiar lying on the ground. I knelt down for a closer look and could hardly believe what I discovered.

"Incredible!" I muttered to myself as I examined a fossil imbedded into a piece of shale. It looked like a seashell, and I knew the elevation where I stood was about two thousand feet above sea level. I was amazed to find something like this lying on top of a mountain near the town of Renovo.

The fossil was from an extinct species of the Brachiopods living on the ocean floor some five-hundred-million years ago! Brachiopods are a class of mollusk-like animals with a pair of appendages, one on each side of the mouth. I was captivated by the engraved image of this fascinating creature, and it made me think about the extraordinary changes that have occurred on our timeworn planet. It seemed so surrealistic; the mountaintop where I stood was once on the bottom of an ocean.

While studying the fossil, I remembered finding a tree-stand nearby, many years ago, that had been baited with corn. I decided to hike to it before nightfall, even though it hadn't been used for several years. Hunting over bait is illegal, and it was possible that the site was being baited once again. I put the fossil in my pocket and walked a short distance into the woods. It felt good to get away from the abandoned strip mine and into the forest, even though my trip to the tree-stand proved to be fruitless. By the time I walked back to my patrol vehicle it was dark.

I patrolled my way back home, as there would surely be messages on my telephone answering machine. I hoped I could get any loose ends tied up so that I could relax on the holiday tomorrow. However, this was the mid 1980's, and state game wardens were expected to be on call around the clock. My home phone number was listed in the phone book and printed in the Pennsylvania Game Commission Hunting & Trapping digest issued with each hunting license. It wasn't unusual to get a phone call about something that would need my attention on the day after the close of any big game season. And this Thanksgiving Day was not going to be an exception for me.

Just before nine o'clock that holiday night my telephone rang, and I had a feeling the caller would be conveying a message of importance. I picked up the phone, and before I could say hello the voice on the other end of the line interrupted.

"John, if a man that held a light on a bear when another man shoots it turns in the man that shot it, do you have to arrest the man that held the light?"

"Who is this?" I insisted.

"It's me…Bucky."

I had known Bucky for several years, and this wasn't the first time I received a valuable tip from him.

"Okay Bucky, tell me what you have."

He told me that a young man staying at a camp near his camp was involved in the illegal killing of a bear. Bucky explained that man was troubled by what he'd done and wanted to confess, provided that he wouldn't be fined. Bucky said that if I agreed not to fine him, he would testify against the triggerman. Shooting a bear through the use of an artificial light was a serious offense, and the violation occurred on Sunday, the day before the season opened.

"Tell him he's got a deal," I said.

I made arrangements to meet with them at my headquarters the following day, at one o'clock in the afternoon. Before hanging up, Bucky told me that the bear was a large cub that had been shot from the camp window while it was feeding on some honey. The bear was killed shortly before midnight, and then taken to the Game Commission Northcentral Regional Office (NCRO) check station Monday evening, the opening day of the season. It was checked in and tagged as a legally killed bear.

After hanging up the phone I began reviewing bear kill reports from the NCRO check station. I knew the general vicinity of where the camp was located because Bucky told me it was very close to his. I also knew that the bear was a large cub, and that it was checked in on the opening day. First, I separated all reports of cubs killed on the opening day in the township where Bucky's camp was located. Then I cross checked the names of those successful hunters against a Bureau of Forestry list of registered camp owners hoping one of them owned a camp near Bucky's. It wasn't too long before I came up with a suspect. A man by the name of Sammy Sundee owned a camp very close to Bucky's camp, and he brought in a ninety-pound cub on the opening day.

On Friday morning, I was bogged down with office work, so I asked my deputy Ranger to snoop around Sundee's camp and look for bait. Later that day, Ranger stopped by my headquarters just before noon and told me that he found corn scattered on the ground, and a tree stump soaked with honey behind the cabin. This information would be very useful if the witness got cold feet and decided not to meet with me.

The day seemed to drag on, and by mid-afternoon Bucky and the informant hadn't arrived. I began to wonder if they would show up, however they were traveling quite a distance, so I wasn't about to write them off just yet. I leaned back in my chair and put my feet up on my desk. *Relax*, I thought, they'll be here soon enough. I closed my eyes and began thinking about the opening day earlier in the week, and all of the work involved in apprehending quite a few poachers who were hunting over bait.

I knew of over thirty illegal bear baiting locations in my patrol district, and I had organized a law enforcement sweep at first light with the help of several game wardens from other patrol districts where there was little to no bear hunting.

I met with Ranger well before sunrise on the opening day, and we set off for one of the baited areas near Pottersdale. Just before the opening hour of the season, we surprised a party of twenty hunters lined up for an organized drive. They were about to spread out and make a push toward several other members of the group who were standing on watch with rifles ready. I knew there was corn behind their camp, less than three-hundred yards from where we stood. I advised the captain of the party they could not move forward with the planned hunt, and that it would be unlawful to hunt anywhere in the vicinity. He pretended to be surprised about the bait, and claimed to have no knowledge of it, but I didn't believe him. The forest immediately behind their camp was heavily saturated with fresh corn kernels, and they surely knew it was baited. Some of the corn could be seen from their property line. Had we arrived twenty minutes later while their hunt was in progress, we would have been issuing citations instead of warnings.

I decided to go to their camp and look for stragglers. I often find that camps baiting bears during the hunting season will organize their hunts out of the same mold of deception. They begin the hunt several hundred yards away from the camp, only to advance toward the camp while knowing full well that bears will be close to an abundant food supply. In larger hunting parties, there are usually a few old-timers that can't or won't walk very far. And they will often be hunting within a few yards of the bait.

As soon as we arrived at the camp I spotted a large pile of corn, apples, meat, beef lungs and lard in the back yard. Then a man came out from behind the cabin and walked toward us with his head cocked to his right in a peculiar manner. As we exited my patrol truck Ranger turned to me and said, "I know this guy."

"Who is he?" I asked.

"Ten Till," Ranger replied.

"I didn't ask for the time, who is he?"

"That's his name. Actually, it's a nickname of sorts."

"What kind of nickname is that?" I asked. Before Ranger could answer, Mr. Till was within earshot and my focus shifted to the bait situation at hand.

"Mr. Till, this property is baited. It's unlawful for anyone to hunt in the vicinity of this camp."

"Oh, that's just some table scraps and stuff," he said defensively.

"Well, it's the 'stuff' that I'm most concerned with!" I said assertively. I then asked if there were any camp members hunting in the immediate area, and he said there were not. As he turned to walk back to the cabin, I noticed a general hunting license and a bear license on his back, and when I glanced toward the cabin, I saw a rifle leaning against the wall beside the back door.

"Wait a minute!" I called as I walked over to the rifle and unloaded it.

"You were standing behind the cabin beside this rifle when we pulled up." I said.

"No sir, I was inside the camp, reading."

"Then why was this fully loaded rifle positioned outside the door?"

"In case someone tried to break in," he claimed.

"Oh, I see, you wanted the intruder to shoot you with your gun instead of his," I answered sarcastically. I knew full well what he had been doing, but I didn't believe I had enough evidence for a conviction in court, which is the criteria I use when deciding whether or not to make an arrest. I gave him a stern warning about the rifle, and we departed. As I pulled away in my patrol vehicle, a bell seemed to go off in my head, and I hit the brakes.

"Ranger, take a walk through the woods behind the camp," I said.

Ranger grabbed a portable radio and headed for the woods while I circled the vicinity in my patrol vehicle. I didn't see anyone, so I drove out to meet Ranger on a muddy dirt road behind the cabin. Ranger was still working his way toward an electric powerline behind the camp, so I parked nearby and waited.

Suddenly it dawned on me: Ranger said his nickname is Ten Till because his head was tilted to the right at Ten o'clock. And Ranger stood right next to me and let me call him Mr. Till! I was trying not to laugh as I snatched the microphone from its rest on the dashboard, but before I could scold him my two-way radio snapped to life. Ranger shouted into his microphone that he found someone hunting on the powerline behind the camp. I quickly hiked down to his location and saw Ranger standing next to a man that dwarfed him in size. Ranger is a big man, but the hunter beside him was of gigantic proportions, surely weighing more than five hundred pounds. He had been sitting on the powerline hoping to ambush a bear while it was on its way to the bait pile only a hundred-and-fifty yards away. He was much too large to keep up with the rest of the men in the drive, so he stayed behind. The portly hunter was clearly taking advantage of the bait, and he subsequently paid a large fine by way of a field receipt.

The Game Law clearly stated that it was unlawful to "take advantage of" any bait while hunting. It didn't specify a minimum or maximum distance one must be from a baited area. A person could be hundreds of yards away in some situations and still be in violation of the Game Law if he is intentionally taking advantage of bait. This is especially true when bear hunting since bears will travel great distances, using the same trail each time to get to a baited area. Eventually the trail or trails can develop deep paw impressions in the ground, as bears tend to step in their own paw print or another bear's imprint each time they walk a well-worn trail. I've seen paw impressions six inches deep on some heavily used trails that led to a baited area. An unscrupulous hunter could take a position along such an easily identified trail, hundreds of yards from the bait, and still be in violation of the Game Law. However, this would be unlawful only if he was aware of the bait.

In some situations, a game warden may post a baited area closed to all hunting, and large tracts of land can be shut down depending on the type of bait and the terrain. This can be particularly unfortunate when camps on state forest land are baiting or feeding. Many acres of the surrounding forest open to the public can be closed to hunting. Even after the bait is completely removed, the posters will remain for an additional thirty days because wildlife had been conditioned to go there for food. Essentially, someone laying bait on state forest land can cause a large area of forest normally open to public hunting to be closed for a month or longer.

After finishing up at the powerline, we proceeded to another bait area. This particular camp had been bringing in stale donuts by the truckload, and several bears were coming in each night. I had information that the owner of the camp was hand feeding some of them. We had to walk across an open field surrounded by woodland to get to the camp. The donuts had been dumped into a large wooden platform a short distance from the cabin. As we looked things over the property owner came out and assured us he was not a bear hunter, and that no one from his camp hunted anywhere in the vicinity. "People come from fifty miles away to look at the bears," he said proudly.

Cub bear being hand fed.

I explained the problem he was creating, and he assured me that next year he would stop feeding two months before the season opened. I would have preferred that he stop altogether, but I was willing to take what I could get. It was illegal to hunt through the use of bait, but anyone could legally feed bears. It would be almost two decades later (2003) that a law was enacted making it illegal to feed them.

Under normal circumstances a bear is not to be feared. They are normally very docile and will often run away when they see or scent a human. However, a bear will lose its fear of humans if it is continuously fed, as it will become conditioned to associating people with food. And if a bear is hand fed, matters can become much worse. Hand fed or "habituated" bears will sometimes roam through rural towns looking for a handout. In addition, they may approach people who are camping, fishing, picnicking, or just walking in the woods. This can be extremely unnerving to say the least. I thanked the man for his promise not to feed during the hunting season and we departed.

I have dealt with bears that lost all fear and respect for humans because of feeding. I remember watching one such bear lying on a porch while eating a large bag of dog food and refusing to move when the door was pushed opened against him, preventing the homeowner from exiting the front door! I've investigated incidents where habituated bears wandered into open garages, demolished porch doors, smashed fences, broke windows, and even attempted to crawl into homes. These bears will sometimes kill dogs that get in their way, and growl at humans that approach them while they are eating. When it gets to this point, the bear is dangerous and usually ends up being shot.

As we walked across the field toward the woods, I spotted a hunter on watch some two hundred yards away. He saw us too and immediately stood up, turned around, and quickly disappeared into the woods. We jogged across the field and into the wooded area, catching up to him near the road. Our short sprint revealed a maze of bear trails within easy shooting distance of where he'd been sitting. The hunter claimed no knowledge of the donuts, even though he was from a camp only a couple hundred yards away. I didn't believe him, and after a brief conversation he acknowledged

43

that bears were feeding on the donuts. He was cited and subsequently pleaded guilty to hunting through the use of bait.

We returned to my patrol truck and headed toward another baited area, but before we could get there, I received a radio call from a deputy who was on surveillance in the Dry Run area of Chapman Township. The deputy, dressed in camo-orange and posing as a hunter, had apprehended someone hunting near some bait hidden under a stand of small hemlocks in an old forest clear-cut. Fish, chickens, pheasants, apples, grain, and molasses had been scattered along a depression in the ground.

I had inspected the area several times pre-season and kept a written and photographic record each time additional bait was placed. I also photographed evidence of bears feeding there, such as claw marks, footprints, and droppings. This can be useful in the courtroom to demonstrate a continued pattern of baiting and proof that it was being consumed by bears. I had documented similar evidence for each of the thirty-plus baited sites that I found prior to the hunting season, a task that kept me very busy during the months of September and October. During those months, I would concentrate on locating illegal bait locations in my district. One of the methods I used was to simply drive to as many camps as I could each day and then step out of my patrol vehicle to check the immediate area for bait. In addition, I would receive tips by telephone, many times by anonymous callers. Although these were few and far between, they always produced results.

I remember one such caller who described a baited area in the headwaters of Boggs Run, a very remote area of my patrol district. I could drive my patrol vehicle part way, and then had to hike in about a half mile. When I got there, I found a lot of bait that was obviously for black bears. There were donuts scattered everywhere, lard was smeared on trees, and ear corn was spread throughout several acres. It looked to me like this would be an area where an organized drive of hunters would push through in order to chase bears from the baited area toward other members of their party standing on watch with rifles ready. A few days before the opening day of the bear season, I returned to the site and found that all of the bait had been eaten. I knew it would be impossible to prove anyone hunting at this location would be aware that it had been heavily baited prior to the season opener. During this period of time (the late 1980's) trail cameras were unheard of. However, I had a small rectangular cardboard box lying in the back of my patrol vehicle. I used my pocketknife to cut a round hole in one end and placed a baseball-sized rock inside the box to add weight. Then I slid the box under an old moss covered fallen tree that was located where the heaviest concentration of donuts had been.

On the opening day of the bear season, Law Enforcement Supervisor Warren "Quig" Stump and I intercepted a large group of hunters putting on a drive through the bait location. We stopped them and advised them that the area had been baited for bears just prior to the opening day of the season. As suspected, they all claimed they had no idea the area had been baited. I gathered the group near the old log where the camera was hidden, reached underneath and retrieved the box. I told them that there was a trail camera inside, and that it had been there for several weeks. I gave the captain of the group a card with my home phone number and suggested that the person who placed the bait should contact me before I had the film developed. And if that person was willing to admit to placing the bait, I would forgive the rest of the hunting party for hunting in an area that had been baited just prior to the opening day of the season, which was a serious violation of the Game Law. No one was willing to say anything at the time, but I was confident that someone would call me later that evening.

I hadn't told Quig that there was only a rock in the box. I thought that if I could convince Quig there was a camera in the box, the hunters would believe it too. During our hike back to my patrol vehicle Quig asked me if he could look at the camera, since it wasn't something that was issued to game wardens at the time. I reached inside the box and handed the rock to him. We both had a good laugh, and Quig said he would never forget it, whether I tricked the hunting party or not.

Later that evening I got a phone call from a member of the hunting party. He was willing to admit to placing the bait in order to save the rest of his men from being cited. So, I was able to make him look like a hero to his friends, while he paid a big fine for baiting. It would have been impossible to convict anyone else in the hunting party with the lack of evidence I had. But I was the only one who knew that, and I was happy with the way things turned out. Any time I could throw the book at someone while making him look like a hero was a good day for both of us.

My favorite method of patrolling for bait was whenever I could climb aboard a Pennsylvania State Police helicopter. I didn't do this often, but when I had the opportunity, I wouldn't hesitate. One day while flying over state game lands with State Police Sergeant Jack Gerrity and Quig Stump, we observed a hunter walking across a field while holding what looked like a dead wild turkey. Since turkey season was closed, I asked Jack to land in the field while the hunter stood by and watched in awe. He had no idea why a State Police helicopter was landing within fifty yards of where he stood. Jack shut the copter down and we stepped out of the cockpit to greet him…and then cite him for killing a wild turkey during the closed season. As I was writing the citation, we heard a shot from a wooded area within a few hundred yards from where we stood. Quig jogged into the woods and found another hunter who had just shot another turkey. We confiscated the turkeys, and I wrote another citation. I was sure this would be a day remembered by all of us.

The picture below is me (left) with Trooper "Roy" Rogers, and helicopter pilot Sgt. Jack Gerrity from August 1993. The primary mission was searching for a murder suspect; however, I was also looking for baited areas during this assist.

While we were on the way to Dry Run, I received another radio call. Law Enforcement Supervisor Quig Stump had connected on one of the bait areas he was working for me. I told Quig I would meet with him on my way to Dry Run. We were there within fifteen minutes, and I briefly reviewed the facts with Quig. The bait, mostly corn, had been placed within twenty yards of a camp and was heavily used by bears. The camp owner was apprehended standing on watch behind the cabin, seventy yards from the corn, in a manner allowing him to easily shoot a bear as it approached the bait. We were able to determine that bears had been approaching from where he stood by the large amount of bear excrement (which was saturated with corn kernels) on the forest floor. Another guest at the camp had been standing on watch farther away on a pipeline while positioned in such a manner that he had a clear shot at any bear that would cross the pipeline to reach the corn. Quig and I agreed that both men should be cited. Quig told me he would wrap things up and then go on to the next bait area while Ranger and I continued on to meet the officer at Dry Run.

By the time we arrived at Dry Run, the deputy had finished his investigation and released the suspect after issuing a citation. He had been dressed in orange hunting gear while posing as a hunter standing near the bait when the suspect slowly walked by him holding a rifle in the ready position.

"Do the game wardens come back here often," the deputy asked the hunter as he passed.

"No, they just stay on the road," he said.

"Good," said the deputy. "There's a lot of bait around here and I don't want to get caught."

"Just do what I'd do," the hunter offered. "Tell them you didn't know about the bait. Then they can't fine you."

With that, the deputy lowered the boom on him. "State Game Warden," he said while displaying his badge. "Unload your rifle immediately."

The hunter complied and a subsequent search of his vehicle turned up several green sacks of grain in his trunk. They matched the same green sacks the deputy found scattered about the bait pile, thereby linking him directly to the violation.

I later discovered this particular hunter had killed a bear with a revolver the year before in the Dry Run area. I was glad he'd been apprehended, thanks in part to an anonymous letter and map directing me to the bait that I had received a month earlier.

Later in the afternoon, we traveled out to the Tamarack Swamp. A cabin near the swamp had placed some beef tallow and clams beside a corn feeder twenty-five yards from the back door. I had visited the camp prior to the season opener, documenting in my written notes that bears were visiting the bait.

It was getting close to sunset as we climbed out of my patrol truck and walked the perimeter of the camp searching for hunters. Soon we came upon a man hunting near the bait, a guest at the cabin, and he knew that bears were coming in to feed there. He was clearly taking advantage of the fact that bears were conditioned to come to the camp to feed. Even though he personally didn't place any of the bait, he was in violation of the Game Law. He paid a heavy fine and suffered a revocation of his hunting and trapping privileges...

$\mathbf{A}$ loud rapping at my front door brought me back to the present. I had been absorbed in thought about the events that occurred on the opening day of the bear season, and I didn't hear Bucky's truck pull into my driveway.

"Hi John!" Bucky cried out as I opened the door. He thrust out his right hand to meet mine in a firm shake.

"Come on in," I said while focusing on the young man standing nervously behind him.

Bucky followed my eyes, then: "Oh yeah, this here is Jim Bob, and he has something he wants to tell you."

I nodded and invited them into my office while Bucky apologized for being late.

"Okay, Jim Bob, tell me what you know," I said while leaning forward on my desk. Jim Bob was very uneasy and having some difficulty deciding just what he should say.

"Come on...out with it; tell me how Sammy Sundee killed the bear cub," I said with a self-assured smile.

"How'd you know Sammy done it?"

"Never mind," I said. "Just go on and tell me what you know."

Any second thoughts Jim Bob may have had quickly vanished and he explained what happened at Sammy's camp.

Sammy had been baiting bears with corn and he saturated a tree stump behind the camp with honey as well. Eventually, several bears became conditioned to feeding there regularly. At approximately eleven-thirty on the night before opening day, Sammy woke Jim Bob out of a sound sleep. Jim Bob was a new member at the camp, and somewhat intimidated by Sammy. Sammy told him there were two bears feeding at the honey and insisted that Jim Bob shine a powerful flashlight on them so he could get a clear shot. After Sammy fired his rifle one of the cubs fell dead, and the second cub scurried up a tree. Sammy handed his rifle to Jim Bob and told him to shoot it but Jim Bob refused.

Afterwards, Sammy and Jim Bob went back to bed for a few hours of sleep, but all Jim Bob could do was lie on his back and stare at the ceiling in wide-eyed disbelief.

Late on the following evening, Sammy took the cub to the bear check station and claimed the bear as legally killed. Then he took it to a taxidermist for a full body mount.

"Jim Bob, will you testify in court?" I asked.

"Yes sir."

Jim Bob had been very upset over what happened at the camp, and I could sense that he was relieved by his confession and his decision to face Sammy in the courtroom.

Immediately after they left my office, I picked up the phone and called Sammy at his home. The conversation went something like this.

"Hello?"

"This is State Game Warden Wasserman calling from Clinton County. I want to talk to you about the bear you shot."

"Sure, go ahead."

"Well, it seems there are some issues with the method used to kill the bear."

"No way! I took it to the check station, and they tagged it as a legal kill, so there's no problem." Sammy was being very assertive now and was shouting into the phone. However, I had all of the aces and decided to show him my hand.

"Killing a bear during closed season, at night, with a light, over bait. Seems like a lot of problems to me," I said in a matter-of-fact tone.

"No way. No way!" he replied defiantly. Sammy was starting to sound like a broken record, and I decided it was time to change his tune.

"Jim Bob just left my office," I said. The telephone line seemed to go dead. There was total silence. Finally, in a very somber tone Sammy asked, "How much is the fine?"

Sammy's hunting and trapping privileges were revoked for several years, he paid a very large fine, and his bear was confiscated.

Throughout my long career with the Game Commission, I dealt with a lot of bears, and bear hunters. Most bear hunters don't violate the Game Law, and I always considered them to be the best of the best overall. Bear nuisance complaints are where I spent most of my time, and they involved as much or more of my attention than chasing poachers.

Black bears will eat almost anything, and that's one of the ways they get into conflicts with humans. They can easily become accustomed to humans, especially if they are fed or find an artificial food source near people. Bears that become accustomed to being near humans are considered "habituated" bears. These are bears that have developed a habit of being around humans and have lost all or most of their natural fear of people.

One of my most memorable experiences with a black bear dates back to 1976, when Merle Goodling called me about a bear that was causing a problem near his home in Hyner. I had only recently graduated from the Pennsylvania Game Commission Training School and had very little hands-on experience trapping bears. However, I did have a state issued culvert style bear trap parked behind my home, and I was anxious to use it for the first time. The trap was essentially a three-foot-wide by eight-foot-long galvanized steel drainpipe permanently mounted upon a trailer frame. The frame included taillights, a license plate, and a two-inch ball hitch in order to mount the entire rig onto my state vehicle. In order to set the trap, it was necessary to attach some bait to a trigger assembly inside the culvert. A small doorway allowed access to the trigger. Once baited I would have to lift the half-inch thick steel guillotine-like door at the entrance of the culvert straight up until a spring-loaded pin snapped out from underneath to hold it in place.

When I pulled into Merle's driveway while towing the culvert trap behind my state vehicle, Merle stepped off his front porch and walked over to my truck. He stood there with his hands on his hips while shaking his head side to side, and then he started laughing.

"You ain't gonna catch any bears in that thing," he with a big grin on his face.

"Hi, I'm State Game Warden John Wasserman, nice to meet you sir," I answered. Merle was still chuckling when he stuck out his hand to greet me with a firm shake.

"I'm going to prove you wrong sir, I have jelly donuts and bacon for bait, and I'm going catch this bear!

"Okay John, if you say so," he said while still chuckling. "Let's get it set up; I'll help you with it." After the trap was set and baited, I asked Merle to call me when a bear was in the trap.

"You mean if, not when," he said with a broad smile.

The following morning at first light I received a phone call from Merle. He said I caught a raccoon, and he could see it scurrying back and forth inside the trap, so I went right over before breakfast to release it. Of course, I had to endure Merle chuckling while he reminded me I'd never catch a bear in my culvert trap. He managed to do it in a good-natured way without being antagonistic, and I couldn't help but like the guy. I released the raccoon, reset the trap, and headed home for breakfast before starting my patrol for the day.

The next morning, I got another call from Merle explaining that I had another raccoon! When I got to Merle's home he was standing by the trap with a big grin on his face.

"I won't say it John," he chuckled.

"You don't have to Merle," I laughed. "But I'm gonna prove you wrong…eventually."

"Okay John, I hope you do. This little guy is running back and forth and chattering, and I think he's trying to tell us he wants out."

I released the raccoon, reset the trap, and spent the rest of the day patrolling the big woods of Clinton County.

The next morning, Merle called once again at first light. This time he told me the trap had been set-off and that it was empty. I grabbed a quick bite to eat and headed out to his home, fully expecting Merle to remind me that I'd never catch a bear in my culvert trap. Merle was sitting on the porch of his hand-built log home while smoking a corn cob pipe when I arrived. I stepped out of my truck and waved to him before walking over to the culvert trap. Merle waved back but couldn't resist reminding me I'd never catch a bear in "that thing" as he described it. There were several two-inch by three-inch rectangular holes in the side of the trap to allow for a "jab-stick" with a syringe to pass through in order to tranquilize a bear. The front and rear of the trap had dozens of two-inch diameter round holes in order to allow for air to pass through. I peeked into one of the larger holes on the side of the trap, and all I could see was darkness. Then I walked around to the entryway of the trap, grabbed the handle at the bottom of the heavy steel door, and started to lift it straight up.

BAM!

It sounded like a gunshot as the trap vibrated and shook from side to side. I had only lifted the door a few inches, but quickly jumped back and fell on my rear as I let go of the handle. There was a huge bear in the trap! When I began to lift the heavy steel door the bear slammed into it with his paw.

The bear was so large that it almost completely filled the inside of the culvert. When Merle and I first looked inside we couldn't see anything but blackness, so it looked like an empty trap, since very little natural light could enter through the holes on its side. Previously, the raccoons had been easy to notice because they were moving and chattering.

Merle jumped up from his chair and ran over when he saw me fall backwards.

"What happened?" he cried.

"A very large and very angry bear happened," I said as I stood up and brushed off my pants.

"Well, I'll be danged. You did it!" Merle mumbled softly while his pipe bobbed up and down in his mouth. "The next time I'll be more careful when I look inside."

"Me too," I said. "I'll never make that mistake again. And there's one other mistake I made."

"Oh yeah, what's that?"

"I should have bet you twenty dollars that I'd catch a bear in that culvert trap," I said with a chuckle.

So, I had this big angry bear in my trap, and I needed to tag it and remove a tooth before I could release it in another location. I was convinced that I could do it correctly, even though this would be the first time I "processed" a bear for the PA Game Commission. I had assisted one other game warden with this procedure during my field training before graduating from the Game Commission Training School. And I grew up hunting, fishing, and running trap-lines in rural Bucks County Pennsylvania during the 1960's. Handling wild animals was nothing new to me.

First, I had to tranquilize the bear. I carefully measured the amount of drug necessary and transferred it into a heavy-duty steel syringe designed for large animals. Then I attached the syringe to a jab-stick, which is an aluminum pole we used to inject the drug. Merle shined a flashlight into the trap so I could see better, and I quickly poked the bear in its rump through a two-inch diameter hole on the side of the trap. At that instant the bear growled, the trap swayed side to side, and the jab-stick almost snapped out of my grasp. It was bent, but the full dose of the drug had entered the bear's hindquarter. After twenty minutes passed, the bear appeared to be sedated, so I lightly tapped its nose with the butt end of the jab-stick. He was out like a light!

I lifted the heavy steel door up until a spring-loaded steel pin locked it in place. He was facing the door when I jabbed him, and he was too large to turn while inside the trap. This made it much easier for me, since I needed to put metal tags in both ears and remove a small tooth.

First, I clamped a numbered metal tag onto each ear so the bear could be identified if it was captured again. Next, I used dental forceps, a special type of pliers, to remove a small pre-molar tooth. The tooth protruded just above the gum line; however, the root was a quarter inch long. I placed it inside a small envelope for our bear biologist to determine the bear's age by cutting the tooth open and using a microscope to count growth rings in a cross section of the root. Merle was fascinated by all of this, and he asked a lot of questions while watching me work on the bear.

Sedated bear. Note the metal ear tag and the size of its head.

After I finished processing the bear, I closed the sliding steel door and hooked my state truck to the hitch on the trap. It was a huge male, and I estimated its weight between five hundred to six hundred pounds.

I transported the bear forty miles away to a site between Keating and Pottersdale and drove down an old trail to a clearing in the forest. By now the bear was wide awake and a little grouchy from the bumpy ride on unpaved state forest roads. When I approached the trap, I could hear his jaws clacking. Bears often do this when they are afraid, and when a bear is afraid it has two choices: fight or flight. Most of the time they choose flight.

I tied a rope onto the door handle and threw the other end on top of the trap. Then I climbed on top of the steel culvert, grabbed the rope, and lifted the door up so the bear could escape. I could see its nose brushing up against one of the holes on the top of the trap while he sniffed and huffed inside. It was a bit unnerving because the bear knew exactly where I was, and I began wondering if he was thinking about a little revenge. Thankfully, after a minute or two, he bolted from the trap and ran into the woods out of sight.

Over the years, I would capture many more bears on Merle's property. Whenever I would be setting a trap, Merle would chuckle and say, "You'll never catch a bear in that thing." And I'd answer with, "Want to bet twenty bucks?" We became good friends, and I remember many afternoons sitting on his porch with him and chatting about whatever came to mind at that particular moment.

Clinton County was, and still is one of best counties in the state for bear hunting, often leading the state with the highest number of bears killed at the end of the season. And back in the 1980's, the sleepy village of Hyner seemed to be a bear magnet.

Not far from Merle's home was the home of Howard Lunger, one of only two or three beekeepers in my district. Howard knew more about beekeeping than just about anyone in the state, and even though he took great precautions, a bear would occasionally get into his hives. Howard would surround his hives with an electric fence in order to keep the bears away, and sometimes he would wrap a bacon strip around a strand of electrified wire, just to make sure the bears would get the message. However, almost every year a bear would manage to get into the hives and damage them. The Game Commission reimbursed beekeepers for bear damage to their bee colonies and hives, and it was my job to inspect the site, verify that the damage was from a bear, and process the claim. I almost looked forward to getting a call from Howard about bear damage because I enjoyed spending time with him and helping by compensating him for the damage to his hives.

Howard was deeply religious, a great trapper, hunter, outdoorsman, ginseng gatherer, and one of the kindest men I've ever known. After inspecting the bear damage, we would retreat to his kitchen, sit down together, and talk about anything to do with the outdoors. Often his wife Grace would join us. She was a soft-spoken, wonderful woman whom I will never forget. After finishing the paperwork necessary for the damage claim, it was impossible to leave without a jar of his best honey. I'll never forget Howard and Grace Lunger, or Merle and Anna Goodling. May they rest in peace.

Black bears love corn, and any farmer in bear county will tell you how much damage they can do to a cornfield. A bear can add up to two pounds of fat per day if it has access to a cornfield, and its body weight can increase up to thirty percent during summer through fall. I remember a man who bought an old farmhouse in Hyner and tried growing a few acres of corn. I wish I could remember his name, but he didn't stay in the area very long, and all I can recall is the number of bears I caught in his small cornfield. Nine bears during a single month, and his cornfield was devastated! I don't think he got much more than a few bushels of corn for his troubles. The picture below was taken about thirty days before the corn was ready to be picked. By the time it was ripe, most of it was either eaten by bears, or they rolled on the stalks to the point where the corn couldn't be used for human consumption.

Hollowed areas in cornfield were caused by bears damaging stalks.

I spent over thirty years in Clinton County, Pennsylvania as a state game warden from 1976 to 2007. I couldn't begin to count the number of bears I trapped and relocated, or the number of bear nuisance complaints I serviced. One of the most severe incidents occurred when a bear tried to enter the home of an elderly woman who lived alone in the tiny village of Bitumen. The bear had damaged some screens in her windows but didn't manage to get inside her home. She was very scared; however, I was able to trap and remove two bears with a culvert trap that I set in her backyard.

Screen window damaged by bear.

Dumpsters tipped by rummaging bears.

Black bears are extremely powerful animals, with rare individuals weighing more than eight hundred pounds. Normally they will not threaten humans, but their strength is not something you want to underestimate.

SHADOWS OF THE MOON

It was December 1978, and the antlerless deer season would soon close as the sun began to sink below the horizon. I drove my patrol vehicle behind a stand of hemlock trees and killed the engine. Now I would watch and listen. I was on the alert for poachers deep inside a five-hundred square-mile section of state forest where homes, telephone lines, and electricity ceased to exist. It would be another forty years before cell phones would have some limited use here.

Nearby, was State Route 144, the Ridge Road, a remote paved highway connecting Renovo (population 1,200) to Moshannon (population 280). One can travel this road for twenty-five miles without encountering any sign of civilization except for an occasional hunting camp.

Twilight would soon be overcome by darkness as I rolled down my window to better hear any approaching vehicles, or perhaps the distant gunfire from a poacher's gun. The frigid air was crisp and stimulating. An hour went by with only three cars passing softly in the dim evening light.

A full moon began rising, and soon I could see shadows dancing on the snow-covered ground. It was a beautiful, quiet night in the middle of nowhere, and I loved every minute of it. And I was getting paid for this!

Well, not really, because back in 1978 there was no such thing as overtime payments for game wardens. I had been on patrol for fifteen hours, since well before sunrise, but I didn't mind; this was a way of life for me and was nothing like the typical job most people are faced with. I rarely took a day off, and I answered calls from my Game Commission telephone whenever I was home, day or night. In those days every game warden's home phone number was listed in the hunting digest issued with each hunting license. Things were less complicated back then, and the digest was so small it fit in your shirt pocket, containing only about fifty pages. Each game warden (game protector) was required to have an office in their home that was open for public business, and expected to conduct that business whenever we were home, within reason. We were not permitted to leave our assigned patrol district without first getting approval from a supervisor, including when we were off duty or on a day off.

To report a Game Law violation, or to participate in the Game Commission's SPORT program, telephone the nearest District Game Protector. If he cannot be reached, contact the Game Commission Division Headquarters having jurisdiction for the particular county involved. For a list of all counties in each Game Commission Division, see Page 53. Addresses and telephone numbers for Game Commission Division Headquarters are found on Page 54.

DISTRICT GAME PROTECTORS

ADAMS COUNTY

Becker, G. W.	Aspers 17304	717-677-
Troutman, J. J.	New Oxford 17350	717-624-

ALLEGHENY COUNTY

Lockerman, S. E.	Pittsburgh 15239	412-327-
MacWilliams, R. G.	Clinton 15026	412-695-

ARMSTRONG COUNTY

Carll, W. E.	Kittanning 16201	412-548-
Scott, A. C.	Rural Valley 16249	412-783-

BEAVER COUNTY

Szilvasi, G. T.	Midland 15059	412-643-

BEDFORD COUNTY

Wylie, T. C.	Woodbury 16695	814-766-
Warner, B. L.	Manns Choice 15550	814-623-
Barney, T. C.	Everett 15537	814-652-

BERKS COUNTY

Goedeke, H.P.	Bernville 19506	215-488-
Snyder, J. J.	Kutztown 19530	215-683-
Schmit, M. W.	Shillington 19607	215-775-

BLAIR COUNTY

Hershaw, H. L.	Hollidaysburg 16648	814-695-
Martin, D. D.	Hollidaysburg 16648	814-695-

46

BRADFORD COUNTY

Bower, W. A.	Troy 16947	717-297-
Rockwell, A. D.	Sayre 18840	717-684-
Gallew, E. N.	Wyalusing 18853	717-265-

BUCKS COUNTY

Bond, E. F.	Fountainville 18923	215-249-

BUTLER COUNTY

Weston, W. N.	Boyers 16020	412-735-
Heade, L. P.	Butler 16001	412-285-

CAMBRIA COUNTY

Jenkins, D. W.	Patton 16668	814-247-
Marks, D. E.	Johnstown 15905	814-255-

CAMERON COUNTY

Erickson, N. L.	Emporium 15834	814-486-

CARBON COUNTY

Burkholder, C. E.	Weatherly 18256	717-427-
Moyer, D. L.	Jim Thorpe 18229	717-325-

CENTRE COUNTY

Snyder, L. D.	Milesburg 16853	814-355-
Wiker, J. L.	Pennsylvania Furnace 16865	814-692-
Mock, G. F.	Coburn 16832	814-349-

CHESTER COUNTY

Fasching, E. J.	Elverson 19520	215-286-
Clark, E. T.	Cochranville 19330	215-869-

CLARION COUNTY

Bower, J. G.	Knox 16232	814-797-
Couillard, G. J.	Clarion 16214	814-226-

CLEARFIELD COUNTY

Zeidler, D. J.	Rockton 15856	814-583-
McGinness, W. A.	Clearfield 16830	814-236-
Furlong, J. R.	Ramey 16671	814-378-

CLINTON COUNTY

Wasserman, J.	Renovo 17764	717-923-2213
Hancock, J. B.	Lock Haven 17745	717-748-

47

61

I was getting hungry, and there wasn't anything happening here, so I decided to head home for a hot meal. Besides, I had made arrangements earlier to meet with an informant, and I didn't want to keep him waiting.

On my way home, I decided to take a short ride down Barneys Ridge Road, an unpaved forestry road that dead-ended at a point on a ridgetop overlooking the West Branch of the Susquehanna River to the north, with the Fish Dam Run Wild area on the west, and Barneys Run on the east. This area could best be described as off the beaten path deep inside the middle of nowhere.

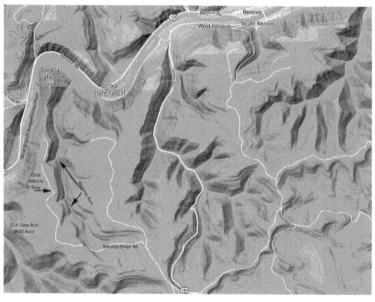

A bright, full moon over the snow-covered ground provided good visibility as I turned off my headlights and proceeded slowly along the narrow road. After rounding a curve, I observed a vehicle a hundred yards ahead of me. The operator was shining a spotlight out the driver's side window. The vehicle was stopped in the middle of the road, so I grabbed my binoculars and looked in the direction where the light was shining. When I brought the lens into focus, I could see a doe illuminated by the spotlight just as it spun around and disappeared deep into the forest.

I snapped my headlights on, and the moment my lights lit up the vehicle ahead of me, the operator turned off the spotlight and sped away. Spotlighting wasn't unlawful, but spotlighting while in possession of a firearm certainly was, and why else would someone turn off a spotlight and race away so quickly?

I turned on my rotating red emergency light and pursued the vehicle, stopping it about a quarter mile away. I could recognize that it was an older model International Scout as I got out of my patrol vehicle and approached it.

"State Game Warden; keep your hands where I can see them," I called out while shining my flashlight on the driver.

The first thing I noticed was a scoped bolt action rifle propped up against the passenger seat with the lens covers flipped up.

"Sir, may I see your driver's license."

"Why? I ain't doing nothing!" said the driver.

"Spotlighting while in possession of a firearm is against the law," I said. "I can see you have a rifle with you."

"I wasn't spotlighting, so I don't have to show you nothing," the driver insisted. "So, why don't you go on your way and stop harassing me?"

"If you're refusing to identify yourself, I'll have no choice other than to place you under arrest."

The driver seemed stunned for a moment. "Arrest me? Are you serious?"

"I am."

He shook his head in disbelief and reached for his back pocket. "Sure, thing officer," he said pulling a wallet from his jeans and extracting a license from inside. "But like I said, I wasn't spotlighting, and I didn't do nothing wrong. You can search my vehicle and see for yourself if you want."

The name on his driver's license was Bill E. Gote, and I couldn't imagine why he was christened as Bill instead of William! I glanced at his face and noticed a long wispy beard growing from underneath his chin near the back of his throat. The front of his chin was clean shaven. A closer look revealed the beard, or goatee, was in two sections that grew together from each side of his jaw line.

It looks like Billy is gonna have a baaaad day, I thought.

I asked him to step outside, and then patted him down to check for a weapon. He was clean, but I decided to handcuff him while I searched his vehicle.

"Sir, I'm going to temporarily handcuff you for my personal safety while I search your vehicle. Soon as I'm done, the cuffs come off."

"What! Why that just ain't right. I already said you could search my vehicle."

"Well, that was nice of you sir, but I don't need your permission. Turn around and place your hands behind your back."

"What if I don't?"

I raised my flashlight so the beam hit him square in the eyes. "Mr. Gote, I want you to think very carefully about what you just asked me. Because you won't like the way I'm about to answer your question."

Mr. Gote stood there for a moment sizing me up. Then he turned and put his hands behind his back. I cuffed him and carefully searched inside the old Scout while I had Mr. Gote stand in front of the headlights.

A closer look at his rifle revealed that it was a .243 caliber, and the attached scope was set at the lowest power. I found a .243 caliber cartridge (live round) on the floor next to the rifle, and two nearly full boxes of ammo in the back of the car. There was a hot wire coming straight out of the dashboard that wasn't connected to anything.

"Where's the spotlight that was connected to this wire?" I asked.

"I don't know what you're talking about," he said. "I told you before that I wasn't spotlighting. There ain't no spotlight, and you better quit harassing me. I'm good friends with State Representative Russ Letterman, and he's gonna get you fired from the Game Commission. You don't know who you're messing with!"

I glanced at his driver's license and looked back at Mr. Gote. "Oh, so you're not Bill E Gote...You gave me someone else's license?" I said sarcastically.

"No, it's my license and you know it is. You mess with me and you'll pay the consequences later when Russ gets done with you."

"You've made your point Mr. Gote. I'll be leaving now. But not before I hand you a citation for spotlighting a deer while in possession of a firearm."

"Uncuff me if you're done searching," he demanded.

"As soon as I'm finished. I can't keep an eye on you and write at the same time."

"You said that I'd be free after you searched my car!"

"You will be soon enough," I said. Then I turned and walked back to my vehicle.

After I finished writing the citation, I grabbed his rifle and the cartridge that was lying next to it for evidence and placed them in my patrol car.

"Hey, that's my rifle you're stealing!" shouted Gote. "What do you think you're doing?"

"I'm seizing it for evidence. You'll get it back when this case is final, either by your guilty plea or a verdict by the court."

"You can't do that!"

"Oh yes I can sir, and I just did.".

I uncuffed Mr. Gote and handed him a copy of the citation with a receipt for his rifle and the cartridge that I seized for evidence.

He looked down at the citation, then whipped his head up and glared at me. "Five hundred dollars! For what? I didn't do anything!"

"Sir, it seems we disagree. I suggest that you ask for a trial and then the judge will decide who's right."

"That's exactly what I'm gonna do. And the next thing I'll do is place a telephone call to my friend Russ Letterman. You're finished! Kiss your career goodbye because he's gonna see that you're fired!"

After I allowed him to leave the scene, I ripped an old rag in two and tied one half to a hemlock sapling where I stopped his Scout, and the other half to a tree limb along the road where I first observed him spotlighting. I was running late for my meeting, and a search for the spotlight would have to wait.

When I arrived home, I contacted my trusty deputy Ranger and explained what had happened on Barneys Ridge Road. I asked him to look for a spotlight between the areas I had flagged with the rags. He was having supper and said he would go out and look for the spotlight as soon as he finished.

Two hours later Ranger arrived at my home holding a spotlight, his face beaming with a wide grin.

"Wow, that's fantastic," I said. "I knew you'd find it!"

"And it gets even better. Look at this," Ranger said as he held up the power cord. The twelve-volt DC cigarette lighter plug that had been attached to the cord was cut off, and the wires were stripped and prepared for a direct hot wire splice in order to operate.

I smiled and nodded my head approvingly. "It doesn't get better that this."

"Actually, it does," said Ranger. "The spotlight was lying lens down on top of the snow, and the snow under the lens had melted."

"So, it was on, throwing a beam of light just before landing in the snow."

Ranger nodded his head, "Exactly. It was definitely generating heat across the lens before he tossed it."

"Perfect…I'll file charges against him first thing tomorrow morning."

Two months later, a trial was held before the district judge in Renovo, and Mr. Gote was found guilty of unlawfully spotlighting for deer while in possession of a firearm. He immediately filed for an appeal of his conviction to the Clinton County Court of Common Pleas. The appeal was scheduled to be heard by President Judge Carson V. Brown seven months later in September.

However, in a desperate attempt to prevent the appeal from being heard, Mr. Gote met with Pennsylvania State Representative Russell P. Letterman. Mr. Letterman represented the seventy-sixth Legislative District of the House of Representatives, which included my patrol district in Clinton County. The meeting was held in the back room of a tavern located in the city of Lock Haven. A few days afterward, Mr. Gote sent a three-page letter to Mr. Letterman where he formally accused me of lying about what happened on Barneys Ridge Road.

That letter was necessary in order for Mr. Letterman to forward an official written complaint to the Pennsylvania Game Commission from Mr. Gote, one of his constituents (a person represented by an elected official).

In the letter, Mr. Gote denied the spotlight was his, denied spotlighting, and claimed there wasn't a live round of ammo on the floor of his vehicle. He stated that I fabricated the evidence by taking a cartridge out of one of the boxes of ammo in his Scout and placing it on the floor. He asked Mr. Letterman for any and all help he could give and stated that he was being persecuted and railroaded. In the letter, Mr. Gote also stated that his appeal of the case was scheduled to be heard by the Clinton County Court of Common Pleas.

Because Mr. Gote had previously been found guilty by a district court judge, and his appeal of that conviction was pending, it was highly improper for Mr. Letterman to get involved at this point. Nonetheless, Russell Letterman sent a letter to Pennsylvania Game Commission Executive Director Glenn Bowers asking him to *"...look into this matter on behalf of Mr. Gote and see what can be done."* He closed the letter with, *"Any assistance you can give will be greatly appreciated by Mr. Gote and myself."*

It was my opinion that the purpose of Letterman's correspondence was to pressure the Game Commission to have the charges withdrawn. Russell P. Letterman was a powerful state legislator with a lot of influence. He was the

Chairman of the Pennsylvania House of Representatives Game and Fisheries Committee. Any amendments in the Game Law or hunting and trapping regulations that the Game Commission desired would first need to be approved by Mr. Letterman.

Mr. Bower's response to Mr. Letterman was in part, *"Since he (Mr. Gote) was found guilty, the evidence presented must have been adequate and well presented. This case is now pending in the Clinton County Court; therefore, any comments would be improper. I am certain whoever hears this case in Clinton County will rule on the matter according to the evidence presented."*

This was a big deal...Mr. Bowers wouldn't budge. He stood up against a very powerful legislator.

Several months later, the Clinton County Court of Common Pleas found Mr. Gote guilty of the charge I filed against him. President Judge Carson V Brown filed a lengthy written opinion explaining that while some of the evidence was circumstantial, he believed my testimony was credible. His opinion in part, *"...a deputy found a spotlight lying face down with the lens approximately six feet off of the roadway with the cord extended towards the roadway. The ground was snow covered where the light was found; however, there was moisture on the lens in the form of water droplets. It was found under circumstances indicating that it had been placed in the snow while it was still warm thus allowing an inference that it had been used and placed there fairly recently and certainly within the time period that the defendant was on the scene. There is no requirement that the firearm be loaded, and in view of the fact that officer Wasserman found ammunition nearby so that the gun could have been loaded in a very short period of time in order to shoot at a big game animal, it could be inferred from the Commonwealth's evidence that the defendant (Mr. Gote) had in his possession a firearm whereby a big game animal could have been killed."*

In an ironic twist of fate, some thirty years later, the Fish Dam Run Wild Area where Mr. Gote was stopped was renamed The Russell P. Letterman Wild Area. This was done by an Act of the PA House Of Representatives. However, to me, it will always be the Fish Dam Run Wild Area, and I'm not alone with that sentiment.

F ast forward fifteen years and I have another unusual story to tell about an incident that happened under the shadows of the moon.

It was a cold December evening back in 1994 when Bill, Ed, John, and Dan piled into Bill's Bronco after enjoying supper at the Mountain Top Inn at Haneyville. While driving back to their cabin, they noticed a two-tone sedan passing in the opposite direction while they were swapping deer hunting tales. Seconds later, their headlights picked up two men hastily dragging a deer across the road toward the Haneyville Baptist Church.

Bill slowed down, and when he was within a few yards of the men, the shadowy figures let go of the deer and ran into a heavily wooded area behind the church. Bill and his friends were close enough to get a good look at the deer, and they could see that it wasn't a legal kill. This was buck season, antlered deer only, and the deer lying on the ground in front of them was a doe.

Bill drove a few hundred yards down the road to a nearby home so they could ask permission to make a phone call. As John stepped inside the house to call the Pennsylvania Game Commission, Bill was watching vehicle headlights that were slowly approaching from the rear. The car slowed, almost coming to a stop by the church, then quickly picked up speed and raced by Bill's Bronco. Bill realized that it was the same two-tone sedan he saw after leaving the Inn, so he immediately gave chase. Within seconds he was close enough to get the license plate number and then he quickly ended the pursuit in order to turn around and pick up John, so they could return to the Baptist church.

When they arrived at the church the deer was gone! Bill turned his vehicle in the direction of a small cemetery behind the church, and then came to a stop in order to light up the area with his headlights. Dan cautiously opened the door and climbed out so that he could look around. Moments later he spotted two men lying down in the cemetery beside the deer!

"There they are!" he yelled. With that, both men got up and ran in opposite directions. One of them passed through the bright beams of Bill's headlights enabling him to get a good look at the suspect. He was able to determine the man was of medium height, weighed about one hundred forty pounds, had dark hair, was in his late twenties, and was wearing blue jeans and a red sweatshirt. At this point, Bill and his friends decided that it would be best to stay put until the Game Commission arrived.

I had been contacted by the Game Commission radio dispatcher, and my deputy Ranger and I were hastily making our way up Hyner Mountain Road to meet with the witnesses. The headlights of my patrol vehicle would rise and fall in concert with every undulation in the roadway as my red emergency lights reflected off the dense forest that embraced us. We knew there was probably little chance of finding the two poachers, but it would not be for lack of trying.

We arrived at the scene at about nine o'clock and had a long discussion with the witnesses. I ran a check on the license plate Bill provided, and it came back to Rocco Rowdkyl from a small town some fifteen miles away (Rocco was the head of a family that had a history of Game Law violations).

I contacted State Game Warden Ron Stout by two-way radio, explained everything, and asked him to visit the Rowdkyl residence while we continued our investigation. Ranger and I discovered that the poachers had dragged the deer into the cemetery and dressed it out after the witnesses left the scene in order to make the phone call. We concluded that the deer had been shot very late in the afternoon or early evening in a field across from the church and hidden nearby until dark. A tactic regularly used by poachers to avoid detection during daylight hours is to shoot a deer from their vehicle, and immediately drive away as soon as the deer drops to the ground. Then they will return in a different vehicle a few hours later, often soon after nightfall.

Whoever was driving the Rowdkyl vehicle had dropped off the suspects, with the intention of returning minutes later, in order to pick them up with the deer.

The poachers saw headlights approaching, and thought it was their accomplice, so they dragged the deer across the road in plain view. But the headlights belonged to Bill's Bronco, as he was just ahead of the accomplice's vehicle!

I suspected that the poachers were still out in the woods somewhere, perhaps watching us as we examined the carcass.

Ranger and I stood by near the church, waiting to hear from Game warden Stout. Thirty minutes passed before he contacted me by two-way radio and said he had a long conversation with Rocco Rowdkyl. Rocco claimed he didn't know anything about the illegal deer kill. In addition, Ron had checked Rocco's vehicle and it was clean.

We thanked the witnesses for their help and suggested that they return to their camp. Then Ranger and I loaded the deer on a steel rack attached to the back of my patrol vehicle and drove away…but not too far away. I pulled in behind an abandoned building, shut off the motor, and we waited. We figured that if we were being watched, the suspects might think we had left the area and that it would be safe to come out into the open.

About an hour passed before we spotted a man walking along the dark roadway in front of us. We quickly approached him on foot and identified ourselves. The man was dressed in a thin jacket, certainly not enough for the cold temperatures we were experiencing in the mid-teens. I noticed some brush on the front of his jacket and thought perhaps he had been lying on the ground. The man identified himself as Sam "Bam" Boozel from the state of Delaware.

"They call me Bam!" he said with a wide grin while nodding his head up and down like a wooden puppet.

He told us a man he had met earlier in the day drove him to a bar several miles up the road, and they had a few beers together. The man (he only knew his first name) later slipped out of the bar and left him there, so Bam decided to walk all the way back to his camp.

"Is that the best you can do for an alibi?" I said.

"I ain't lying." he insisted. "I even bought him a few drinks and he up and leaves me there with no way to get back except my own two feet."

We handcuffed Bam and put him in the back seat of my patrol vehicle, and then drove to the bar in order to verify his story. As I suspected, the bartender didn't remember him at all. However, Bam wouldn't budge from his story and insisted that he had been at the bar earlier that night.

I realized that he wasn't going to admit anything, so I had no choice other than to take him to his camp, a mile from the crime scene, and release him.

I slowly crept up the gravel driveway to his camp and stopped my patrol car.

"Okay Bam, get out, but you'll be hearing from me again," I said.

"What do you mean by that?"

I told him we didn't believe his story, and that it was ridiculous. Then I said, "When I'm finished with this investigation, you will be getting a citation for your part in the unlawful killing of a deer."

"I don't think so," he chuckled as he exited my patrol car. "You ain't got nothing on me."

He was right. We didn't have any evidence connecting Bam Boozel and his accomplice to the illegally killed deer. And we didn't have a clue as to who the accomplice was. All we had was a description from our witness that the man we wanted was on the smallish side while in his mid-twenties with dark hair and wearing blue jeans and a red sweatshirt.

After Bam got out of my patrol car he walked toward his camp: a log cabin that appeared to be shut down, in total darkness.

"We gave it our best John," Ranger said wistfully.

"Yep, I thought he'd crack when we took him to the bar and the bartender said he'd never seen him before."

We were just about to leave when Bam walked into the cabin and turned on the lights. There, through a cabin window, we watched as he frantically raised his arms with palms forward as though signaling someone to stay put. But it was too late, for a man wearing a red sweatshirt suddenly appeared through the cabin window.

Ranger and I were on the front porch within seconds. I hammered on the door with my fist, and soon Bam let us inside with a look of serious concern on his face. I told Bam to step aside so I could get a better view of the man in the red sweatshirt. Just as I suspected, he was wearing blue jeans and matched the description of the second suspect provided by our witnesses.

"I'm with the State Game Commission," I said. "What's your name?"

"None of your business," the man grunted. "And you can get out of my cabin right now. I didn't invite you inside."

"We have reason to suspect that you were involved with an illegally killed deer," I said. "You can save yourself a lot of trouble by cooperating with us."

"So, what if I don't, what are you gonna do, arrest me?"

I reached for the handcuffs on my belt. "Only if you make me."

"Whoa! Take it easy, man," he said, taking a step back. "Name's Robby Rowdkyl! What's this all about?"

"We just want to ask you some questions."

I wanted to separate the suspects for questioning at this point, so I asked Robby to step outside with Ranger. As he turned to go out the door, I noticed the tip of a leather knife sheath protruding from just underneath his sweatshirt. I immediately stopped him and removed the knife from the sheath. There was fresh blood on the blade. I acted like I didn't notice it and set the knife aside on a nearby table. Ranger glanced at the knife and then did a quick pat-down search to make sure Robby didn't possess any other weapons.

Ranger seated Robby in the passenger seat of my patrol car and questioned him while I remained in the camp with Bam.

I looked squarely into Bam's eyes, "Listen Bam, when you're caught, you're caught; are you man enough to admit it?"

This line of questioning can work well under the right circumstances with the right person, as I'm mildly provoking him by insinuating that I may doubt his manhood.

Bam puffed out his chest. "Darn right I'm man enough!"

Bam told me what I wanted to know, and everything happened just about the way we figured it did.

Robby shot the deer just after sunset and left it lay. A few hours later, Robby's father Rocco took Bam and Robby back out to retrieve the deer and dropped them off near the church. The witnesses spooked everyone, and they split up. Bam said he would pay whatever his fine was, but he wouldn't testify under oath in court against Robby.

"He's done hard time in the slammer," Robby said nervously. "He's nobody to mess with. Same with his dad."

I thanked Bam for his confession, grabbed the knife off the table, and walked outside to see how Ranger was making out. However, Robby would only say that he had dressed out a buck deer for another hunter earlier, and that's how the blood got on the knife, so I decided to try "trickery" in order to elicit a confession from him. This is a legitimate law enforcement tactic as long as the officer isn't using coercive methods in an attempt to get an admission of guilt. The easiest way to understand this is if the trickery isn't something that would pressure someone to make a false confession, it's lawful.

"Listen Robby, Bam just told me everything. Said he'd testify in court. I know you shot the deer. The best thing you can do right now is start telling the truth."

Often, this tactic will work, but Robby was an ex-convict familiar with police tactics. He wouldn't budge from his story that he had dressed out a buck for a stranger earlier in the afternoon.

A perfect alibi, I thought to myself, and it would be impossible to convict Robby in a court of law because Bam was unwilling to testify against him.

"Let him out of the truck Ranger, we're done with him…for now."

I held on to Robby's knife and a hunting rifle that we found in the camp as evidence, and then I issued a citation to Bam in the amount of five hundred dollars.

Now…How do I deal with Robby? I had to try something new, something that hadn't yet been done in Pennsylvania. During this time period, DNA evidence was a new emerging science for solving wildlife crimes. Actually, it was still rather new for solving crimes involving human beings. However, perhaps it was time for Pennsylvania to begin using this technique to convict poachers.

The use of DNA (Deoxyribonucleic acid) evidence to convict a human of a crime had only first occurred six years earlier and was still considered a relatively new science. The first person in the United States to be convicted of murder using DNA evidence was twenty-five-year-old Timothy Spencer, who was also known as The Southside Strangler. Spencer was a serial killer who committed three murders in the state of Virginia, all during the fall of 1987. He was executed six years later on April 27, 1994, only eight months before my investigation began.

The use of DNA to solve wildlife crimes was largely unheard of during this investigation back in December of 1994. However, I had recently read an article in a wildlife magazine about The United States Fish and Wildlife Service Forensic Lab, located in Ashland, Oregon. It had only been in existence for a few years and was created to help put a stop to illegal exports and imports of products made from endangered wildlife, as well as protected natural resources. It seemed like the lab was capable of doing almost anything when it came to forensic determinations concerning wildlife.

I carefully packaged and shipped Robby's blood-stained knife, and a separate blood sample from the illegally killed doe, to the serology department of the forensic lab for comparison. The lab was capable of determining if two or more blood samples are from the same animal, and I hoped they would be able to confirm the blood on the knife came from the deer in the graveyard.

Several weeks later I received a report from the lab indicating that there wasn't enough blood on the knife to provide a sufficient sample to determine whether or not both blood samples were from the same deer. However, the lab did determine through DNA analysis that the blood on Robby's knife was from a female deer.

Shortly after receiving the report from the forensic lab, I filed charges of unlawful possession of a deer, and dressing out game in a cemetery against Robby. (Ranger and I had cleaned up that mess, as it would have been intolerable to leave blood and guts near a tombstone).

Meanwhile, Bam pled guilty to his charge of unlawful possession of a deer and paid the fine. Only that single offense had been filed against Bam because he was cooperative.

Robby, however, decided to plead not guilty and asked for a court trial. He refused to talk to me, and he wasn't interested in anything the Forensic Lab had determined. Shortly afterwards he ended up in the Clinton County Prison on a Burglary charge, where he would remain until the day of his trial on the Game Law offenses.

I was able to catch up with Bam while he was at his camp a few weeks before the trial date. He claimed he couldn't remember much of what he told me the night of the crime and said jail would be a better option than testifying against his friend. Nevertheless, I served him with a subpoena to appear at the trial in Lock Haven.

I believed I had a strong circumstantial case even if Bam failed to appear in court to testify. Robby had been discovered in a camp within one mile of the crime scene. That camp was owned and occupied by Bam Boozel, who previously had pled guilty to possessing the doe. A vehicle that had been cruising slowly by the crime scene was registered to Robby's father. Robby closely fit the description of one of the suspects and possessed a knife with fresh bloodstains from a female deer. He lied to Ranger about the origin of the blood, claiming it was from a buck that he helped someone dress out. This can be argued in court as "consciousness of guilt". In other words, the defendant lied because he was aware of the fact that he was guilty of committing a crime.

The charges had to be proven beyond a reasonable doubt, and the defendant had the right to ask questions during the trial. So, I couldn't merely introduce the written report from the Forensic Lab into evidence at the trial. I needed to have the examining scientist come to Pennsylvania and testify.

I contacted the lab and talked to James LeMay, the forensic scientist who conducted the DNA analysis. Jim had been with the National Fish & Wildlife Forensics Laboratory since it first opened. Jim assisted in the development and verification of the analytical DNA procedures necessary to positively identify wild animal parts back to their species or gender. He was also responsible for forensics examinations on a wide range of complex and difficult wildlife parts and products originating from endangered, threatened, or regulated species. It seemed like Jim was just the man I needed. I asked Jim if he would come to Lock Haven, Pennsylvania to testify, even though I believed he would refuse because of the distance, time, and expense involved with flying more than two thousand miles across the country from Oregon.

Jim didn't hesitate. "Yes, of course." He said.

As it turned out, Jim was anxious to testify in a Pennsylvania court because he had not yet been declared an expert witness by a judge in this state. It would be his first case here. Once declared an expert witness by a Pennsylvania court, it then carries tremendous influence with other Pennsylvania courts. Because of their expertise, a judge or jury will give weight to an expert witness's words.

The price tag of DNA testing and subsequent testimony by a forensic scientist traveling across the country can cost many thousands of dollars. And the Game Law empowers officers to bring civil action in court against a defendant on behalf of the Commonwealth to recover the costs of such expert testimony.

When the big day finally arrived, Robby was escorted to District Judge John Frazier's courtroom by two sheriff's deputies. He was dressed in a dazzling fluorescent orange jumpsuit with an elegant stainless-steel bracelet adorning each wrist connected by a short chain.

Normally, I would have presented the evidence to the court. However, the County District Attorney decided to prosecute the case, as DNA evidence had not yet been used in Clinton County for humans, let alone for wildlife. Several county attorneys were seated in the courtroom to observe because this case was so unusual.

As I expected, Bam didn't appear, and a warrant was later issued for his arrest.

However, Bill, Ed and Dan did appear for the trial as witnesses, and they did an excellent job of testifying about what they observed on that dark, cold December night.

Next, it was my turn, and after being sworn to tell the truth, I testified about my involvement in the investigation and the arrest of the defendant.

We saved the best for last, and James LeMay was called to the stand as our final witness. The first question the district attorney asked Jim was to explain to the court why he should be declared an expert witness concerning DNA evidence.

Jim spoke at length about his education and scientific background. He was only part way through his testimony when the judge interrupted.

"I've heard enough, and I hereby declare you will be considered an expert witness on this subject in my courtroom."

Jim glanced at me, and we both smiled. And then Jim explained how he concluded that the blood on Robby's knife was from a female deer. There wasn't anyone in the courtroom who could fully comprehend what he was saying about how isoelectric focusing and protein staining for glucose phosphate isomerase, superoxide dismutase, erythrocyte acid phosphatase and albumin proved that the blood samples he examined were from white-tailed deer.

But it surely did sound impressive!

Jim concluded his testimony by stating that the use of electrophoresis revealed that the blood on the knife was from a female deer.

Robby Rowdkyl never knew what hit him. Like a punch-drunk fighter he wearily rose from his seat and admitted his guilt. Jim LeMay's testimony was irrefutable, and Robby knew it.

My case was immortalized by the US Department of the Interior, in a 1997 report to Congress as "the first DNA Game Law case in the history of Pennsylvania successfully prosecuted as a result of forensics support from the US Fish & Wildlife Laboratory."

Today The U.S. Fish and Wildlife Forensic Lab serves one hundred eighty countries who signed the United Nation's CITES (Convention on International Trade in Endangered Species) Treaty, and all fifty states in the US. It has also assisted the International Criminal Police Organization (INTERPOL) with forensic analysis.

Patrolling the Yukon

It was a wet bone-chilling forty-eight degrees as I waited for a taxicab at the Anchorage International Airport in Alaska back in 1995. It was quite a contrast from the mid-August heat wave I had become accustomed to that summer. The temperature had reached ninety-nine degrees just before my flight departed from Pennsylvania, and the cold rain pelting my face was a jolt of Alaskan reality. It was the first day of a three-week adventure that would soon take me to the Yukon Territory and my friend Torrie Hunter, a game warden headquartered in Dawson City.

Initially, I would spend ten days in Alaska exploring such places as Willow, Talkeetna, and Denali National Park. There would be long days and short nights, with sunsets beginning about 10:30 p.m., followed by ninety minutes of twilight. Nightfall would come just before midnight, lasting only five hours before the sun peeked over the horizon again. In Alaska, the farther north you are, the days become longer in summer and shorter in winter. In Barrow, two hundred seventy miles north of the Arctic Circle, the sun doesn't dip below the horizon for eighty-four days from May through August.

In late August, after spending a week in Alaska, I departed from Anchorage and headed for Dawson City Yukon, a distance of five hundred miles. After driving over three hundred miles on two-lane roadways, I finally reached Tetlin Junction. A sign on the road said, DAWSON CITY 165 MILES with an arrow indicating a left turn. By now I was road weary and anxious as I began the last leg of my journey.

I turned left onto the Taylor Highway and stopped dead in my tracks. A dirt road! Worse yet, another sign stated there was road construction for the next twenty-five miles. And to top it all off, still another sign stated that the Canadian border would be closed from eight o'clock that evening until eight the following morning. I looked at my watch and figured if the construction didn't hold me up too long, I might arrive at the border in the nick of time. The race was on!

The hundred-mile trip to the border was dusty and jarring. I only had five minutes until eight o'clock rolled around. I was about one mile from Canada, and I clenched the steering wheel as I sped for the border crossing. Suddenly an awful thought entered my mind: what if the border closed at eight o'clock *Canadian time?* Since Canadian time was one hour ahead, that would make it almost nine o'clock there!

I hit the brakes and slowed down moments before cruising into Poker Creek, Alaska, population two, elevation over four-thousand feet. This is the northernmost border port in the United States Customs firmament. I stopped at the border crossing gate with only minutes to spare and prayed that a guard would soon arrive to open it. Moments later, a uniformed woman with two little children stepped out of a nearby log cabin. The kids stayed on the porch while mom walked over to my car, and after a few brief questions about my purpose for visiting Canada, she opened the gate and I crossed into the Yukon.

The Yukon Territory covers over two-hundred thousand square miles with a population of only thirty-seven thousand people. To put it into perspective, Pennsylvania encompasses forty-five thousand square miles with a population of approximately thirteen million. Clinton County Pennsylvania, considered remote by most Pennsylvanians, has nearly the same population as the Yukon crammed into nine hundred square miles.

The Top Of The World Highway, from the US – Canadian border to Dawson City may be the best unpaved road in the North. It's wide, smooth, and fast. It was sixty-five miles to Dawson, and I didn't pass a single vehicle, home, or cabin. I finally dropped down out of the alpine tundra of the White Mountains and reached the Yukon River by ten o'clock. After a brief wait, the George Black Ferry transported me across the mighty Yukon River to Dawson City. The ferry was capable of handling eight vehicles, but I was the only passenger on this trip. Of all the destinations in the North, Dawson is the most famous because of its wild history during the gold rush of 1897-1898. Today Dawson has a population of about thirteen hundred with most of the town restored to the look of the original gold rush days.

Dawson City Historical Complex

I was relieved to have finally reached my destination, and I could clearly understand why the hundred and sixty-five-mile stretch from Tetlin Junction to Dawson City was closed from fall through spring due to heavy snows.

Dawson City is quite small, and Torrie's home was easy to locate. I found myself on his doorstep knocking softly at about ten-thirty in the evening. A moment later, Torrie opened the door and greeted me with his usual charismatic smile displaying two rows of pearly whites. Torrie stands about six-foot-five, and I craned my neck to greet him as I thrust out my palm for a firm handshake. Torrie had been in Dawson City for ten years, and he patrolled a thirty-thousand square mile district. In comparison, the average Pennsylvania State Game Warden's district is about three hundred square miles.

Torrie invited me inside and introduced me to his wife Nancy, and then we discussed plans for the following day. We would be patrolling the Yukon River in a motorboat and decided a good night's sleep was a must. I was looking forward to sleeping in a bed for the first time in ten days, as my Alaskan nights found me in a sleeping bag, either camping in a tent or in a rustic log cabin on Byers Lake near Denali (Mt. McKinley), the highest mountain peak in North America.

The next morning, we were dressed in bulky one-piece orange survival suits and on the Yukon River by way of Torrie's powerful patrol boat. The river is wide, fast, wild, and unforgiving. Although it was August, the morning air was a chilly thirty-two degrees, with the water temperature not much warmer. The Yukon River is over two thousand miles long, the fourth longest in the world. Silt from glacial runoff causes the river to appear a chalky gray, and unreadable depths add to the mystique of this awesome, often forbidding watercourse that no roadway parallels. We traveled twenty miles before coming upon our first person on the river. A man in a canoe had just floated ashore on the opposite bank a short distance downstream from our position. We maneuvered our boat toward the bank and drifted ashore to talk with him. The man had traveled to the Yukon from Japan, and once here, he purchased an old handmade canoe in Teslin, near the British Columbia line. His destination was Circle Alaska, some eight hundred miles from Teslin. He was unhappy with the heavy weight of the canoe, and intimidated by the fast current of the river, so he stayed close to the bank on his trip. We wished him luck, and as we continued downstream Torrie remarked that each year people drown while on the Yukon River, and sometimes their bodies are never found.

We traveled another twenty miles before we spotted two people cautiously paddling a canoe close to the opposite bank, and we made our way over to them. I was surprised to learn they were from Milford Pennsylvania and had traveled to the Yukon for a vacation. After a pleasant conversation with them we continued downstream. As we neared the confluence of the Fortymile River, Torrie pointed to a Peregrine Falcon on the ledge of a sheer mountain wall. Then we saw another Peregrine gliding high above us. A peregrine can reach a speed of more than two hundred miles per hour in a vertical dive called a stoop. (*The Peregrine was an endangered species in the United States at the time*).

"Ready for lunch?" asked Torrie.

I nodded favorably and we slowly drifted to shore at the mouth of the Fortymile River. After securing the boat, we hiked a short distance through the woods to the abandoned village of Forty Mile. Most of the log structures that made up the town still stood, although they were slowly being swallowed up by an ever-growing forest. I was amazed at how well preserved the buildings were, and Torrie explained that the dry Yukon climate was the reason.

Abandoned Church at Forty Mile. Circa 1886

On August 17, 1896, George "Siwash" Carmack struck gold in the Klondike Valley in extraordinary quantities. He and his partners, Tagish Charlie and Skookum Jim, staked three claims and then hurried off to file them in Forty Mile, located a half day's journey down the Yukon River. Carmack displayed his vial of large new nuggets to everyone he met, and Forty Mile, with a population of about one thousand people, was deserted the next day. Everyone moved to Dawson City, and many "Forty-milers" struck it rich as they were the first of the "stampeders" to stake and file claims. Stampeders was the name used during the Klondike Gold Rush to refer to the thousands of men, and a few women, who were rushing towards the gold fields.

Torrie and I ate our sandwiches on the bank of the Fortymile River while sipping coffee poured from a stainless-steel thermos. We watched two flocks of Sandhill cranes pass overhead, followed by a bald eagle that flew less than a hundred yards above us. *(The bald eagle was endangered in the US at the time. The first photograph of a Sandhill Crane nest in Pennsylvania didn't occur until fourteen years later)*.

After lunch, we set out for a fish camp a few miles downriver. The afternoon sun warmed the air, and it was actually quite comfortable as we continued our journey down the Yukon River. Before long, I spotted a log cabin on a high bank several hundred yards downstream, and Torrie identified it as our next stop. It was occupied by three men who spent the entire summer catching salmon for a livelihood.

A flat bottom boat was moored against a makeshift wooden pier just below the cabin, and we pulled against it. Velvet covered antlers from a freshly killed moose were lying in the boat. Moose season was open, and while Torrie was examining the kill tag, we heard two high power rifle shots on the other side of the river.

Torrie jumped back into the patrol boat, and we sped across the river in the direction of the shooting. Soon we spotted a boat that had been pulled onto the bank of a small peninsula and Torrie pulled ashore beside it. After securing our boat, we followed a pair of human footprints along the muddy riverbank, and soon came upon the tracks of a wounded moose. Blood splatters near the hoof prints were dry, so we knew it had been shot the day before. We stayed on the trail and soon came upon some wolf tracks that were wider than my hand. They were the first wolf tracks I had ever seen other than photographs and drawings. I stopped for a moment to examine them, and then shifted my gaze to the surrounding mountains enshrouded with black spruce, white birch, poplar, and aspen. The sun was shining from a bright blue sky, and patches of brilliant yellow leaves were interspersed with the dark greens of spruce. It was a moment I will never forget. It was wild. Exhilarating!

"Come on, there's two hunters ahead." said Torrie.

My trance was suddenly broken. I looked downriver and saw two men standing on the shore beside a fallen spruce tree. We approached them, identified ourselves, and Torrie began asking questions. We discovered that a day earlier, one of them had wounded the moose we were tracking. It was a large bull, and he also fired the two shots we heard earlier at the same animal. After checking their licenses, we assisted in tracking the wounded moose into the woods. Unfortunately, the blood trail soon disappeared, and there were no hoof prints to follow once we got away from the soft terrain near the river.

We stuck with it for a while, but with no blood and no tracks it was useless. We wished them luck in finding the moose and departed in order to resume our journey down river. Five or so miles downstream we pulled ashore at a log cabin perched on a high bank that was barely visible from the river. It was occupied by Torrie's French-Canadian friend Gayton. Gayton ran down the bank to greet us and Torrie handed him his mail and newspapers. We readily accepted an invitation for a cup of coffee, and I was introduced to his dog Mooshka, a large, energetic husky. We walked up the steep bank to the cabin that had been hand built by Gayton many years ago. It was small but sturdy, with a sod roof, and I had to duck my head as I walked through the doorway.

Once inside, Gayton lit a gas stove to heat up some coffee. A small fire was burning in the wood stove, as the August nights could be very cold. The interior of the cabin was dimly lit, as sunlight filtering through the thick forest allowed very little light to penetrate the two small windows on each side of the cabin.

I sipped a cup of hot black coffee and learned that Gayton was employed for the summer by the Yukon Department of Fisheries and Oceans to tag salmon running the Yukon River. At other times he earned a living as a master wood carver, specializing in beautiful lifelike sculptures of waterfowl. As we talked, I noticed a small television sitting on a wooden shelf behind me.

"Surely you can't get television reception here?" I said.

Gayton grinned, "I have a generator and a VCR...I watch rented movies." *(VCR-videocassette recorders could record or play back movies.)*

All he had to do was travel sixty miles upriver by boat to rent them, not a great distance by Yukon standards.

After an enjoyable visit with Gayton, we continued downriver a few miles and came upon a wall tent on the west bank of the Yukon. Mary Ellen was the occupant's name, and she was tagging salmon for the summer. Her wall tent, a wood frame structure covered with heavy canvas, had a gas stove for cooking, a refrigerator, and a wood stove for heat.

We were invited inside for coffee, and Mary Ellen showed us an electronic device that could trigger a satellite beamed alarm to Whitehorse, four hundred miles away, for an air rescue to her location. "Don't push any buttons," she laughed as she passed it over, "it'll cost me two thousand dollars."

After a brief chat, we followed her boat out to a fish wheel in the Yukon River. A fish wheel is a huge device that resembles a watermill, designed to allow the current of the river to rotate it while it picks up fish. Capture baskets are built into the wheel at an outward-facing slant with an open end allowing the fish to slide into a holding tank where they could be collected. Checking the wheel, we removed an eight-pound chum salmon and a thirty-pound Chinook salmon. Both were tagged and released.

Fish wheel on the Yukon River

A large salmon ready to be released.

After saying good-bye to Mary Ellen, we continued downriver another ten miles or so to the Alaskan border. By now we had just enough time to return to Dawson City before dark, so Torrie turned the boat around and we began our return journey. Sunset wasn't until almost ten o'clock in late August, followed by one hour of twilight. Torrie told me that from the last week of May until the first week of August, Dawson experienced twenty-four hours of light each day, although a few of those hours were twilight.

We drifted into Dawson at eleven o'clock with just enough light to see the water. We had traveled almost two hundred miles round trip and found only two hunters on the river. Torrie explained that sometimes he would make that trip without encountering any hunters at all, even though big game season was open.

The next morning, we were out the door at first light and on our way to the Dempster Highway in Torrie's patrol vehicle, a four-wheel-drive Chevy pickup truck with emergency lights, siren, two-way radio, and a winch. The Dempster Highway is one of only two public roads on the North American continent that crosses the Arctic Circle. It is a four-hundred-sixty-mile unpaved road that crosses taiga forest (sparse and stunted black spruce, dwarf shrubbery such as willow, and swampy areas known as muskegs) and permafrost-patterned tundra. The Dempster passes the Ogilvie and Richardson Mountain ranges before ending at the Northwest Territories city of Inuvik, near the Beaufort Sea. It is an unparalleled wilderness driving experience. The highway goes through some of the most remote territory in North America, inhabited by moose, grizzly bears, Dall sheep, mountain goats, caribou, lynx, marten, wolverines, and wolves.

There are about four thousand wolves inhabiting the Yukon, however they are seldom seen. Torrie told me he only sees them three or four times per year. This was the animal I wanted to photograph more than any other.

Before entering the Dempster Highway, we filled up with gasoline, as the next vehicle service station was over two hundred miles away. We had traveled a short distance when we encountered freezing rain, and it was another sixty miles before we passed the first human dwelling: an outfitter's ranch.

A little farther up the road we came upon two people fishing for Arctic grayling in the Blackstone River, one of the most beautiful freshwater fishes found in the Yukon. Its most striking physical features are the large, sail-like dorsal (back) fin and colorful body markings. Their dorsal fins are usually fringed in red and dotted with large red, aqua, or purple spots and markings. Arctic graylings' backs are usually dark. Their sides can be black, silver, gold, or blue, while a band of gold forms a border between their sides and white bellies, which are in sharp contrast to their pelvic fins striated with iridescent orange, red, or pink.

Several more miles up the road we arrived at Two Moose Lake, a relatively small body of water surrounded by low elevation moist tundra. We were quick to notice two gyrfalcons chasing ducks over the surface of the water. However, the gyrfalcons seemed to be merely harassing the ducks, as they would cut the chase at the moment I expected a strike to occur. The largest falcon in the world, the Gyrfalcon often chases down ptarmigans in flight while plummeting from the sky at speeds up to eighty miles per hour to strike its prey to the ground. They are capable of taking incredibly sharp turns in the air to attack their quarry thanks to their pointed wings.

Gyrfalcon by John J. Audubon - Public Domain Image

Just beyond the lake we noticed some ravens on the edge of the road, and they flew away as we approached. Torrie said there had been a cow moose with a calf at the lake, and the presence of the ravens was concerning. We drove over to the spot where the ravens had been, pulled over, and climbed out of the truck. Torrie found a bloodstained rag down an embankment, and we suspected there might be a moose kill nearby. It was unlawful for licensed hunters to hunt within one kilometer (two-thirds of a mile) of the Dempster Highway.

Several more ravens were perched near a thick stand of dwarfed willow a hundred yards away, and we suspected a carcass could be found there. However, Torrie advised against entering the area due to the possibility of a grizzly bear lying in concealment. He told me that it would be a legal kill if a native Indian shot it. Native Indians were permitted to kill an animal just about anywhere in the Yukon, in or out of season, as long as it is used for subsistence.

We continued up the Dempster to Lee Bolster's ranch nearly eighty miles from where we first entered the roadway. Lee invited us in for coffee and told us he was seeing a lot of grizzlies while flying. One day in particular he observed sixteen. Lee had a ten-thousand-square-mile government outfitting concession, giving him the exclusive right to guide non-resident hunters there.

After visiting with Lee, we headed back up the Dempster, and after traveling about thirty miles, we met a highway worker who told us a native Indian from the Fort McPherson area (Northwest Territories) shot a cow moose with a calf at Two Moose Lake. He said that the Dawson Indians, specifically the Han Band, would send a letter to the Fort McPherson Indians (Tetlin Gwitchin band) to complain about the kill. Apparently, this was a territorial band issue, and they were also unhappy that a cow moose with a calf was killed.

We continued our journey up the Dempster, passing through some of the most beautiful and remote wilderness in the world. After traveling over two hundred fifty miles, we finally arrived at the Eagle Plains Lodge, located just below the Arctic Circle. The last occupied dwelling we had encountered was Lee Bolster's ranch, one hundred seventy miles back. We filled up the truck with gas, had a great meal, and got a good night's sleep at the lodge.

The next morning, we drove up the Dempster to the Arctic Circle. The Arctic is the northernmost region on Earth and includes the geographical area within the Arctic Circle. The tundra was a beautiful red, green, and gold carpet ending abruptly at the base of the Richardson Mountain Range fifteen miles to the east. A blue sky with puffy white clouds seemed to beckon me to cross the tundra and climb those mountains. Perhaps another day, as this time a carefully composed photograph would have to suffice.

Along the way, Torrie received a radio report that the McPherson Indians were hunting caribou at the Northwest Territories border. Between fifteen hundred and two thousand caribou are legally killed for subsistence along the Dempster Highway by native Indians each year. We continued driving until we reached the Northwest Territories border without seeing any hunting activity. We were now at Torrie's patrol district boundary, so we turned and headed back to Dawson City over three hundred miles away. We had only covered about twenty miles, when an adult gray wolf crossed the road ahead of us. It was the black color phase, and I frantically began assembling my camera gear for what I thought would be a distant shot of a wolf trotting off into the horizon. I was wrong. The wolf only went about thirty feet before finding a discarded caribou hide, and promptly lied down in the tundra to chew on it.

I quickly attached my camera onto a window tripod as Torrie eased his truck up the road until we were directly across from it. The wolf stopped chewing for a moment and looked directly at me with bright yellow eyes. Its mouth was open, baring large white canine teeth, its ears pointed and erect. The wolf stared straight through me, no fear, almost sinister in appearance. I was fortunate to capture this on film, and when projected on a large screen, the image will sometimes cause a viewer to subconsciously place a hand near their throat.

The wolf quickly lost interest in me and turned away to continue chewing on the hide. A siren blast from Torrie's truck failed to get its attention. Torrie said that it may have never seen a human before and had no reason to fear us.

Soon the wolf stood up and gracefully pranced across the tundra to another caribou hide about fifty yards away. I climbed out of the truck with my camera and continued to photograph the wolf as it wandered out farther from me. It would stay about a hundred yards away, apparently deciding this was my limit. All too quickly, the wolf loped across the vast tundra, glancing back only once just before it vanished from sight. I will never forget the fire in its eyes.

We reached Dawson City by ten o'clock that night. In two days, we had traveled over six hundred miles, coming upon only two people who were fishing and without checking any hunters. My concept of remoteness had been altered forever.

The next morning, we were out of the house at zero-dark-thirty and arrived at the Dawson City airport at first light. We had packed our gear the night before, so today we would fly into the bush via Torrie's Piper Super Cub airplane. Torrie was going to hunt for Dall sheep and invited me to go along with him. After loading our gear and de-icing the plane, we took off for the Heart River, a hundred miles away. We were flying at an altitude of nearly seven thousand feet over some of the most rugged terrain I had ever seen. Many of the mountain peaks were capped with snow at our eye level or just above. After about one hour of flight Torrie pointed to our runway, a flat spot of bumpy terrain adjacent to the headwaters of the Heart River. During the flight, we hadn't flown over any roads, camps, or any other sign of human habitation, and I was happy to climb out of the tiny seat directly behind Torrie and stretch my legs.

We were located near an abandoned silver mine along a nameless tributary of the Heart River. It was a beautiful valley surrounded by steep mountains carpeted with willow and black spruce that vanished above the tree line at about two thousand feet in elevation. The tree line is the edge of the terrain where trees are capable of growing. Beyond the tree line, trees cannot survive the environmental conditions (extremely cold temperatures, snowpack, or lack moisture).

We began setting up camp, and a good hot cup of coffee was first on the list, so we quickly started a fire and went about putting up my two-man backpacking tent.

The author with Torrie Hunter near the Heart River

It is unlawful to hunt for six hours after landing in the bush (any region not connected to the road network or ferry system), so Torrie was glassing the mountains while I began photographing some of the scenery. Torrie was watching some Dall sheep near the top of a ridge when a grizzly sow suddenly exploded into view. The bear made a rush for the sheep, but they scattered before she could reach them. Two cubs followed closely on her heels. We watched them with Torrie's spotting scope while the sow began to dig up ground squirrel burrows. Ground squirrels provide a major portion of the grizzly and wolf diet in the Yukon.

Soon it was time to begin the Dall sheep hunt, so I loaded my backpack with photographic equipment, and we began our trek up the steep mountainside. We spooked the grizzly near the first ridge, and she ran away from us with her cubs in hot pursuit. I was glad they ran in the opposite direction of our campsite. We continued our search for a full-curl Dall ram while trekking across the tundra toward the next ridge top. A full-curl ram will have the tip of at least one horn that has grown through three hundred sixty degrees of a circle as viewed from the side.

Late in the afternoon, we crawled on our bellies to the edge of a ridge and saw two trophy bull moose in the valley below us. We stalked them to within two hundred yards and I photographed both animals. Torrie had a moose tag and could easily have shot either of the immense bulls, but there's no way we could have packed out the meat.

The larger of the two looked every bit of twelve hundred pounds, and we were several hours from camp over rugged terrain with an airplane already loaded to near capacity. Before long the moose caught our scent and trotted across the valley out of sight.

We began working our way back to camp and eventually did come upon some sheep within shooting range, but none were adult full-curl rams.

Just before descending the high country, I paused to take one last long look at our surroundings. All I could hear was the wind and the gentle rush of a stream below us. For the first time in my life, I believed that I may have walked upon terrain that no other human had before me.

The author is on the right with Torrie Hunter

We reached the valley floor by eight o'clock that evening with several hours of daylight remaining. As we hiked back to our campsite, I saw fresh moose and wolf tracks and some very recent grizzly scats.

When we arrived at camp, we built an open fire for warmth and used it to cook our supper. It was twilight when we finished eating, and we sat by the fire swapping game warden tales while waiting for the stars to appear. The night sky finally settled in with brilliant stars and a clearly visible Milky Way. It was a dead calm…We were truly alone.

The next morning, we were up at first light and loaded our gear in Torrie's plane. Torrie's Super Cub raced down a bumpy gravel bed before gaining enough speed to lift off, and soon we were flying only a hundred feet above Waugh Creek. From there, Torrie would fly alongside sheer mountain walls and then suddenly skim just over the tops of jagged peaks. This was seat of the pants bush pilot flying, and it made me appreciate life a little more once we finally landed.

After returning to Dawson City, Torrie and I said our goodbyes and I spent the next three days driving back to

Anchorage, Alaska to catch a flight back to Pennsylvania. Along the way, I fished in some absolutely beautiful streams and rivers. Late in the afternoon I would set up my tent and make camp. Fish would always be on the menu for supper. It was a trip I will never forget.

Black Lightening

I was on foot patrol in the Fish Dam Run Wild Area during May of 1995 when I encountered a hunter who spotted a creature that hadn't existed here for over a hundred years. He was hiking back to his car after an unsuccessful attempt at bagging a spring gobbler when we met on the Chuck Keiper Trail. The trail was named for Charles F. Keiper who served as the state game warden in my patrol District of Northern Clinton County from 1951 until his death in 1973 (I was assigned to the district in 1976).

Chuck was a dedicated and well-liked warden, and the trail is a tribute to his devotion to protecting Pennsylvania wildlife. It is a long-distance backpacking trail that goes through some of the wildest and most remote state forest land in Pennsylvania, offering incredible solitude.

The hunter I met was wide-eyed and nearly out of breath when he saw me.

"Officer, I just saw a strange animal back in the woods; it was black with a long tail and incredibly fast!"

"Okay, so don't keep me in suspense, what did you see?" I asked him. I had a pretty good idea what the animal was before he described it, since we had reintroduced fishers into the area five months earlier. I thought perhaps he only had a fleeting glimpse of one, but the story he was about to tell me was familiar yet incredible.

"I was concealed behind some brush using my turkey call," he said, "when suddenly what looked like a cross between an otter and a black mink ran headfirst straight down the trunk of a large oak tree, leaped to the ground, and sprinted toward me."

"It was a fisher," I said.

"A fisher?"

"Yes, we released a number of them recently."

"Well, this fisher thing stopped right in front of me when a gray fox came charging out of a laurel patch on my right and ran full tilt toward this creature! The fisher sees it, but it waits until the fox is only a few feet away before it takes off like a streak of black lightening through the woods! I watched these two critters for at least five minutes, and it looked like the fisher was playing a game with the fox. The fisher would climb up a tree, but instead of staying where it was safe, it would run headfirst down the other side of the tree and leap down to the ground so the fox could chase it again. Sometimes it would ease up so the fox could get within inches of it before taking off again with the most amazing speed and agility I ever saw. It even doubled back toward the fox one time and then leaped onto a tree at the last moment with the fox almost biting its tail. Finally, they both disappeared out of sight, so I don't know how it ended."

I thanked the man for his eyewitness account of a fisher sighting, as it was the first I had heard of since the December release, other than a few of my own personal sightings. His story was fascinating, and I would never have believed it if I hadn't witnessed a similar incident a few months before. And just like the hunter's encounter, the fisher and the fox vanished into the forest, leaving no trace. In my opinion an adult male fisher would have no problem killing a gray fox, and it's possible, in each case, the fisher was preparing to do just that. Perhaps the fisher's strategy was to fatigue the fox, and then move in for the kill.

Once, while hiking in the Adirondack Mountains of New York, I came upon a large fisher attacking a small juvenile coyote. I spooked the fisher, and it ran off, as did the coyote. However, the coyote was seriously injured, and I expected that the fisher would circle back to finish it off.

Sixteen years earlier, I had suggested reintroducing fishers into Pennsylvania by writing a letter to my supervisor. I was certain that they would survive and reproduce, and I thought my patrol district would be a suitable location. However, my request for the reintroduction was denied due to concerns of a fisher/turkey conflict. The agency was troubled by the idea that fishers would prey upon turkeys, and that a considerable number of Pennsylvania sportsmen would be opposed to the reintroduction of a predatory animal to the state.

COMMONWEALTH OF PENNSYLVANIA
PENNSYLVANIA GAME COMMISSION
P.O. BOX 1567
HARRISBURG, PA. 17120

February **COPY**

Proposed release of fishers

Mr. Charles M. Laird, Supervisor

John Wasserman
John Wasserman
Dist. #3-18-1

    I am interested in reestablishing the fisher in the Northern Clinton - Southern Potter County area. I have a location in mind that I feel would be suitable to the fisher. This location is known as the Hammersly Wild Area comprising of some 31,000 acres of rugged, limited access terrain. On the map it would basically consist of the Hammersly Fork Creek and the surrounding headwaters (Hammersly Fork, Tamarack, Conrad, Short Run quadrangles). The point of release I have in mind would be the head of Beech Bottom Hollow (upper right corner of Hammersly Fork quadrangle). This area is interspersed with old growth and mature Hemlock and White Pine. The largest Hemlock is 139 inches in circumference. The Bureau of Forestry does not anticipate doing any timber harvesting in the Hammersly Wild area.

    I understand that some states have been successful in reestablishing the fisher. I feel that if the fisher can survive anywhere in Pennsylvania it would be the Hammersly Wild Area. Prior to the logging era the martin and fisher were plentiful in the head waters of Hammersly Fork Creek. In a book first published in 1903 (<u>Fifty Years a Hunter and Trapper</u> by E. N. Woodcock), a famous old trapper writes of the many fisher and martin that he trapped in this region during the late 19th century. I realize that the timber has changed since then, but the rugged terrain is still the same. This is still a vast, inaccessable area with only a few small villages on its perimiter. The Hammersly Wild Area is in the center of approximately 2,000,000 acres of continous forest land mostly State owned.

My letter to Supervisor Laird in 1978.

The fisher's name is believed to have originated from the animal resembling a European polecat named "fichet." Also known as the fisher cat, it is the second largest member of the weasel family in Pennsylvania, with only the river otter being greater in size. The wolverine, found primarily in isolated reaches of boreal forests and subarctic alpine tundra of the Far North, is the largest land-dwelling member of the weasel family worldwide.

Fishers are long-furred creatures with a lengthy body, short legs, and a tail that measures about one third of the animal's entire length. The fur color is dark to deep brown on the upper body, and black on the tail, legs, and rump. In dimly lit forests, they often appear to be all black in color. However, at close inspection, one will notice tri-colored guard hairs that change from gray near the skin, to dark brown or black medially, to blond near the tip, surrounding the face and shoulders creating a golden or silvery sheen there.

Variation in overall body color can range from light brown to almost black, with some having white patterns on the underbelly. Fishers have five toes on each foot with semi-retractable slightly curved nails. They have the ability to turn their hind paws nearly a hundred eighty degrees allowing them to climb head-first down trees.

Adult males weigh up to twenty pounds, and adult females up to about ten pounds. Males are longer than females and can obtain a length of up to four feet including the tail. Fishers are able to hunt their prey within the forest canopy and on the ground. Squirrels, chipmunks, and mice make up a large part of the food source for fishers in Pennsylvania. However, they are well known for hunting and killing porcupines. Naturalist Roger Powell, Professor Emeritus of North Carolina State University, and author of *The Fisher: Life History, Ecology & Behavior,* found that attacks to the porcupine's face were the initial assault. Then once the porcupine had been killed or subdued with these initial bites, the fisher will flip its prey over and eat it belly-first. Powell writes in his treatise The Fisher (1993), "Fishers are uniquely adapted for killing porcupines. Fishers are built low to the ground, at the level of a porcupine's face, and can, therefore, attack a porcupine's face directly. They are large enough to inflict a substantial wound when they have a chance to bite a porcupine's face, and yet they are small enough to be quick and agile and dart in and out at a porcupine's face while avoiding the porcupine's tail. No other predator has the ability to attack and kill porcupines that a fisher has."

Female fishers give birth to several kits during late winter or early spring with den sites usually located in standing dead tree cavities. Fisher kits weigh only a few ounces at birth and reach about one pound within two months after birth. Upon reaching only four or five months of age, fishers are able to attack and kill small prey animals. They are born to kill!

A juvenile fisher. Photo by the author.

Fishers were distributed throughout most of Pennsylvania prior to the logging deforestation that occurred during the 1800's and up to about 1915. The last remnant populations were in the northcentral counties. By the very early 1900's they were extirpated (eliminated) from the entire state.

So fast forward to 1994, and the Game Commission decided to take another look at reintroducing fishers to the state. However, there was still concern from the agency that some sportsmen would be opposed to the idea. This concern was so great that the agency initially only gave conditional approval to the reintroduction of fishers. A feasibility study would first be conducted, including public outreach programs. My belief at the time was, and still is, that the fisher is a native species to Pennsylvania and should continue to exist here.

One of the largest sportsmen's groups in Pennsylvania at the time was the Unified Sportsmen of Pennsylvania. Donald R. Clemmer co-founded the Unified Sportsmen of Pennsylvania where he served as president for decades fighting for hunting and civil rights. He was a good friend of mine, and he lived nearby in the village of Hammersley Fork with his wife Susan (Kinney) Clemmer. We would talk often, either by phone or in person, and I have vivid memories of his rough, gravelly voice, and some of our intense debates. We didn't always agree on wildlife management issues, but he was willing to listen to what I had to say, and he valued my opinion. Some of our debates would probably be better described as wildly enthusiastic arguments. I believe that's why Don gave me the nickname "Wildman," as he often addressed me using that term while grinning warmly.

Donald was interested in the fact that fishers preyed on porcupines, as these quilled rodents can cause big problems for a hunter's dog if it tangles with one. Often, a dog will get a mouthful of quills and won't learn from the experience. So, it's not uncommon to see them back at the vet being treated time and time again.

In winter, the porcupine's diet consists mostly of twigs and the inner bark of trees, especially evergreens such as hemlock and white pine. However, they are also known to gnaw on wooden buildings, as many cabin owners can testify. Porcupines are attracted to anything salty. Winter road salt can entice them to chew on certain automotive parts, especially those made of rubber such as radiator and heater hoses.

So, the fact that fishers will kill and eat porcupines was almost enough to nullify Donald's uneasiness about the reintroduction of fishers to Pennsylvania. After all, they are predators, and some small game animals would be killed by fishers, so he wasn't convinced that the reintroduction would benefit Pennsylvania sportsmen.

However, when I mentioned that fishers would kill and eat coyote pups if they had the opportunity, I captured Donald's steadfast attention, especially when I told him about the time I'd witnessed this taking place while hiking in the Adirondacks.

Coyotes prey upon deer, while not to the extent that some people believe. However, the fact that they kill *some* deer is enough to put them on the "most wanted list" for many Pennsylvania sportsmen.

There are a lot of coyotes in Pennsylvania, and for the most part they don't have any natural predators here. So even if the prospects of a fisher getting into a den of coyote pups was remote, it was the icing on the cake I needed to convince Donald that the release would be a good thing.

It's not so much that we needed the approval of Donald Clemmer, or the Unified Sportsmen of Pennsylvania in order to move forward, but it was highly beneficial to have him and the organized sportsmen supporting us on such an endeavor.

Donald R. Clemmer went to be with the Lord on April 6, 2010, at age seventy-one. He was a good friend. I'll never forget him.

Toward the end of 1994, I was told that the fisher reintroduction was approved by the Board of Game Commissioners. I was elated that my patrol district was selected for the first release of fishers in Pennsylvania. The northern Clinton County release site was largely based on collaboration between the Pennsylvania Game Commission and Pennsylvania State University project coordinator Dr. Thomas Serfass. After it was announced that my patrol district was selected, I suggested the head of Splash Dam Hollow in the Fish Dam Run Wild Area as the release site. After careful consideration by Dr. Serfass, that location was approved for the relocation.

Trappers in New Hampshire and New York were contacted by the Game Commission and asked to capture fishers in box traps during their respective fisher trapping seasons. The trappers were paid a hundred dollars for male and a hundred and fifty for female fishers. Obtaining the fishers from trappers and transporting them to Pennsylvania was coordinated with the New Hampshire Fish and Game Department and the New York Department of Environmental Conservation. The captured fishers were shipped by air to State College, Pennsylvania. Penn State graduate student Denise Mitcheltree, who was a member of the reintroduction team, transported the fishers from the airport to the Pennsylvania State University (PSU) for pre-release care and clinical evaluation.

Denise Mitcheltree with a tranquilized male fisher.

While at PSU, the fishers were held captive and caged individually for a minimum of two weeks to several months in climate-controlled rooms to facilitate: 1) quarantine as a precaution against infectious disease; 2) treatment of capture related injuries; 3) conditioning on a high caloric diet; 4) collection of blood samples; 5) comparison of responses to various tranquilizing drugs; and 6) evaluation of immune response to canine distemper vaccine.

Dr. Serfass was concerned that the initial fisher release at Fish Dam Run in mid-winter could be problematic. His concern was that some of the fishers may not be able to find enough natural prey species to survive if they would remain close to the release site for an extended period of time. So, in order to counterbalance a potential loss of some fishers due to the lack of an adequate number of prey species, a plan was devised to supplement their natural food source.

I was asked to collect road-killed deer and store them near the release site. Over a period of a few weeks, I collected as many carcasses as I could and hid them near a vehicle parking area overlooking Fish Dam Run.

On December 19, 1994, the day finally arrived when fishers would be released into my patrol district. It was a big day for me personally, as this was something I wanted since way back in 1978. I would often think about E.N. Woodcock's writings at the turn of the twentieth century, and his stories about trapping fishers and martens in Clinton and Potter Counties. Interestingly, he would usually capture more pine martens than fishers, and the marten was another member of the weasel family I hoped would be brought back into Pennsylvania someday. But today was all about the fisher, and I was overwhelmed that this once eradicated animal would be reintroduced to my patrol district.

Dr. Serfass and his team did a wonderful job of public outreach, and the fisher release was a big deal. I was amazed at the large turnout (perhaps fifty) of newspaper reporters and volunteers from all over Pennsylvania when we met at the Fish Dam Run Overlook. From there, I escorted everyone to Splash Dam Hollow on the southwest side of Fish Dam Run.

We had twenty-three of the furry creatures, a mix of males and females, curled up inside PVC tube cages, and plenty of volunteers to help carry them the short distance from our vehicles to the edge of the hollow. After the cages were set down on the snow-covered ground, everyone was asked to back away and remain quiet.

Dr. Serfass and Denise Mitcheltree carried two cages up front and gently set them down on the snow-covered ground in order to allow for newspaper photo opportunities.

Dr. Serfass motioned for Game Commission Region Director Willis Sneath to step behind one of the tubular cages. He would release one of them. My heart was pounding with anticipation.

Everyone standing in the background raised their cameras in preparation for the first fisher to dart out of its cage and into the forest. A hush came over all of us. It was dead quiet except for a few barely audible whispers from the press.

And then Denise turned around and looked into my eyes with a delicate smile.

"Would you like to release this fisher?" She whispered.

I was momentarily stunned! I could understand having the Game Commission's north-central region director release one of the fishers. He was the boss-man. But I had only played a small part in this historical event. Dr Serfass and Denise had done a tremendous amount of work in order to get to this moment in time.

"Yes," I responded. "That would mean a lot to me."

Denise didn't realize that her act of kindness was something I would never forget. She was aware of my letter from 16 years earlier. I had briefly mentioned it to her one day in conversation, but it wasn't something that we discussed at length.

I stepped up to the second cage and knelt behind it. The snow-covered ground was cold, very cold, but I hardly noticed. All I could hear was the faint sound of camera shutters clicking nonstop in the background.

Willis and I opened each fisher's cage door simultaneously. The fisher in Willis' cage shot out like a streak of black lightening. Then the fisher in my cage was out like a flash, running beside fisher number one. The crowd of news reporters and volunteers broke the silence with loud cheers.

Thirteen of the released fishers had expandable radio collars attached to their necks. After the remaining fishers were released at Splash Dam Hollow, Denise Mitcheltree would spend many days and hours tracking them using radio telemetry.

I assumed Dr. Serfass planned to ask some Pennsylvania State University students to help distribute the deer carcasses I collected by dragging them into and around the perimeter of the Fish Dam Run Wild Area. I couldn't imagine how else we could accomplish such a challenging task. But Dr. Serfass had a better idea. A game plan most folks would never have imagined or considered to be at our disposal.

Dr. Serfass asked the Army National Guard if they could provide a helicopter to help get the deer carcasses into the remote Fish Dam Run Wild Area, consisting of about four thousand acres of roadless forest. The deer drop was largely precautionary in case heavy snow would prevent the fishers from finding natural prey.

I had thirty of them stored and ready for distribution. In addition, The Pennsylvania Fish & Boat Commission donated a hundred pounds of fish from one of their hatcheries. Fish were not considered part of a fisher's normal diet. But it was also precautionary.

Shortly after the fisher release, a fifteen-million-dollar twin-rotor Ch-47 Chinook helicopter landed in a clearing near Dennison Ridge, overlooking the Denison Fork of Fish Dam Run. This is where I had the road-killed deer and fish stored in preparation for the flight. This was a light load for a helicopter capable of carrying twenty-six thousand pounds of cargo.

I had plenty of help standing by from Game Commission and Bureau of Forestry personnel. As we loaded the deer onto the helicopter, Denise Mitchletree stood at the edge of the snow-covered ridge and used radio telemetry equipment to pick up any signals from some of the radio collared fishers. She located a male three miles from the release site. Part of her master's degree in wildlife and fisheries science would require that she radio-tracked the collared fishers throughout the winter.

Deer being loaded into Chinook helicopter.

After the deer and fish were loaded inside the helicopter, several Game Commission personnel along with Dr. Serfass and grad student Mitcheltree were escorted to seats in the cargo bay. I was most familiar with the terrain where the deer would be dropped, so I sat on a small jump-seat between the pilot and copilot. After the pilot reviewed emergency protocols with me, the twenty-five-ton, dual rotor, ten-thousand-horsepower behemoth slowly lifted off the ground. A row of windows in front of and underneath the pilot and copilot made it easy to see where we could safely drop a deer carcass.

We flew about one hundred feet above treetop level, and I would give the command when to throw a deer out the back of the cargo bay. This gave a whole new meaning to the word *reindeer*, as deer were falling from the sky all over the

Fish Dam Run Wild Area that afternoon. Two Army National Guard soldiers were positioned and tethered at the end of the open cargo bay, and they would grab a deer carcass and throw it out of the helicopter. The 140 miles per hour wind caused by the twin rotors fitted with six huge fiberglass blades caused the deer carcasses to quickly vanish underneath the helicopter.

The initial release of fishers went smoothly, but that was just the starting point. The radio-collared fishers would need to be tracked for at least the next several months. I offered to act as a guide for Denise Mitcheltree, as I had been patrolling the release area for two decades. We spent a lot of time working together over the winter months, and our mutual love of nature and the outdoors culminated in love for each other. We were married six years later on December 18, 1999, at the edge of a hollow overlooking the Fish Dam Run Wild Area. It was just me, Denise, and the preacher in the middle of nowhere...deep inside the middle of nowhere.

Pennsylvania's present day fisher population is largely the result of a joint project (1994-1998) between the Pennsylvania Game Commission, the Pennsylvania State University, and the Pennsylvania Department of Conservation and Natural Resources. During that period, 190 fishers were reintroduced in six sites in northern Pennsylvania, with the first release in the Fish Dam Run Wild Area of Clinton County.

No Closed Season

In March of 1982, a meeting was held in Harrisburg, Pennsylvania between law enforcement agents of the Pennsylvania Game Commission (PGC) and special operations agents of the United States Fish & Wildlife Service (USFWS).

During the initial and subsequent meetings, plans were put together for a joint undercover investigation focused on the unlawful sale of wildlife in Pennsylvania and surrounding states. Intelligence information revealed that violations were in progress that involved the unlawful killing and sale of wildlife, migratory birds, and fish. Covert special agents from the PGC and the USFWS were assigned to the investigation. Their mission was aimed at identifying and arresting the people who were engaged in those unlawful acts.

The following story is one of many that could be told.

A fake wholesale grocery store named "Southeast Seafoods" was established as a front in southeastern Pennsylvania for part of the investigation. It was focused on the unlawful taking and sale of striped bass along the eastern seaboard. However, it was also deemed to be useful for investigations concerning the unlawful sale of wildlife.

Six months after the initial meeting took place, a USFWS undercover special agent met with Pennsylvania state game wardens in Williamsport where he was given a list of names and other information about poachers suspected of the large-scale killing and sale of deer. The undercover agent was using the fictitious name, Clint Hammer.

After a few unproductive visits to bars in the Williamsport area, Clint traveled to Renovo and stepped inside Joey's Bar on a warm mid-August evening.

It was dimly lit like most barrooms in Renovo, and a thick haze of cigarette smoke filled the air. The room was small with several tables along the walls, and an L-shaped oak bar counter hemmed by ten barstools. A few men were seated on the stools, while a dozen others were seated at the tables. At the back of the room a hulking figure with a Mohawk haircut sat at a table while arm wrestling two stocky men at the same time. He held them steady with his right arm while glaring at Clint, then he slammed his arm down to the table defeating both challengers.

"Flatlander!" he snorted aloud while eyeing Clint. Everyone in the room chuckled dutifully.

Clint nodded at the behemoth, then looked at the bartender. "Buy that man a drink," he said loud enough for everyone to hear. Then: "No…buy *everyone* a drink; they're on me!"

Clint stepped over to the bar followed by a chorus of cheers from the patrons. Pulling out a stool, he sat next to a thin, middle-aged, bearded man wearing a black ball cap.

"Thanks for the beer," the bearded man said. "Nobody does that around here…but then, you're not from around here, are you?"

"Just passing through," Clint responded. "By the way, who's the guy with the Mohawk? He doesn't seem too friendly."

"He ain't. That's Big Nasty, and it's probably a good thing you bought him a drink." *(Authors note: This event occurred years before Big Nasty beat alcoholism).*

"Good to know. By the way, my name is Clint, what's yours?"

"Sonny…Sonny Day."

"Well, thanks Sonny, I appreciate the warning about the big guy."

He called the bartender over and laid a hundred-dollar bill on the counter. "Drinks are on me as long as I'm here."

The bartender swiped up the bill and stuffed it in his shirt pocket. "You got it, my friend."

Clint nursed his beer while Sonny drank one after another. Thirty minutes later, Sonny had downed a half-dozen bottles of Budweiser and was feeling pretty chummy toward Clint. They started a conversation, and Sonny told Clint he worked at a tavern named the Belch Bar near Williamsport, and that he was in Renovo visiting a friend. After a few more beers, Sonny and Clint started talking about deer hunting, and before too long, Sonny introduced his friend Spin, seated next to him and drinking just as heavily. Spin told Clint that he'd been listening to their conversation all along but didn't want to speak until he was sure Clint wasn't a game warden.

Clint looked at him for a long moment, then said, "What makes you think I'm not?"

Sonny and Spin exchanged nervous glances. Then Clint slapped his hand on the counter and started laughing. "Gotcha!" he said. He pulled out another hundred-dollar bill and laid it on the counter. "Do I look like some dopey game warden to you?"

"Nope!" said Spin. "Game wardens don't have that kind of money." Then he ordered two more beers for Sonny and himself."

Spin told Clint that he made extra money by taking in hunters from the Philadelphia area and providing food and lodging at his home. He said he would fill tags (kill a deer) for five dollars per antler point. Clint gave Spin and Sonny his Southeast Seafoods business card, and they made arrangements to meet again. Sonny suggested that he stop by the Belch Bar.

"Call the bar first to make sure I'm there," added Sonny. "I'd like to talk to you about something."

As Clint was leaving, Big Nasty finished off his tenth beer, then ripped off his shirt and began climbing up on the bar.

Everyone scattered.

A few weeks later, Clint made a visit to the Belch Bar to talk with Sonny. As soon as he stepped inside, Sonny motioned for him to walk over to an unoccupied section of the room. Sonny told Clint that he didn't want to interfere with Spin's business when they first met in Renovo, and that he was able to supply the agent with deer.

"I can supply you with plenty of deer," he assured him. "Way more than Spin could ever dream of getting for you."

Sonny bragged that he had been selling deer for the last twelve years, that he had a place to properly store them, and that he gets $1.50 per pound for each deer carcass, dressed and skinned.

"That's good to hear," Clint said. "Call Southeast Seafoods when you have something for me, and we can do business." They shook hands and Clint turned around and walked out of the building.

One week later, USFWS Special Agent Abraham, who was assigned to answer any incoming calls to Southeast Seafoods, received a phone call from Sonny Day. Sonny advised him that he would be able to furnish five or six deer by the end of the week. He said that he had a place to store them and keep them cool until pickup. They would be skinned and dressed, and the price would be a $1.50 per pound as agreed to. Special Agent Abraham said that the pickup would be arranged, and that Clint Hammer would contact him by phone to finalize the details.

A few days later Clint placed a telephone call to Sonny and asked him how many deer he had. Sonny said that he only had two deer so far, but that he'd be able to get more soon.

"I'll take them now," Clint said. "How about we meet tomorrow morning in the parking lot behind the bar?"

"Sounds good to me," Sonny replied enthusiastically.

When Clint arrived the following morning, Sonny's truck wasn't in the parking lot, so he waited. Soon two men walked out of the building and approached him. The first was a tall thin man wearing a black cowboy hat; the other was short and stocky with shoulder-length black hair and a full beard. The man wearing the cowboy hat identified himself as Killian. "We've got some venison for you," he said. "They're in my truck, skinned and frozen solid."

At that moment, Sonny pulled into the parking lot, stopped his truck, and walked over to the group of men.

"Sorry I'm late," he said. "I tried to get another deer for you on my way here but there were too many people out and about."

The short stocky man introduced himself as Bubba and said, "Anything else you want? We can get you bear, turkeys, antlers in velvet, just about anything. We've been supplying deer meat to a couple of bars around here; you never know what's in their hamburgers." He started laughing hysterically.

Clint told them he was interested in whatever they could get for him. "But we gotta be careful," he added. "This stuff I'm buying will be shipped out of state, so it's a violation of both state and federal law."

Bubba started laughing hysterically again. "We ain't worried about that. We've been doing this for years. Never been caught, not even close. Game wardens around here ain't too smart."

Clint smiled in agreement. "Yep, you got that right. I've been buying all over the east coast for years, and those federal boys are even dumber."

That remark caused all of them to howl with amusement, especially Clint.

Bubba said they estimated the weight of the two deer at one hundred fifty pounds, which amounted to $225 at the agreed-upon price. Clint handed the money in cash to Sonny and told him to call when they had more venison available. Everyone was happy with the transaction, especially Clint Hammer.

One week later, Sonny contacted Clint and said he had two more deer ready for pick up. The next morning, Clint met Sonny, Killian, and Bubba in the Belch Bar parking lot. The deer weight was estimated at one hundred twenty-five pounds, and Clint handed Sonny $190 in cash. Bubba told the agent that he could supply him with illegal bear hides for $50 each and that he does about $20,000 worth of business each year in M-80's, cherry bombs (illegal in Pennsylvania and many other states), and half sticks of dynamite.

Sonny told Clint that he usually takes his wife and son with him while poaching with his truck as he feels it is less suspicious. He went on to say that he also kills deer from his motorcycle, skins and quarters them, and then transports the meat in a cooler on the rear of the motorcycle. He bragged that he recently killed a bear that weighed over four hundred pounds and sold the meat to some of his customers.

Clint looked at his watch. "I gotta be on my way. Before I go, I want to remind you guys to be very careful and keep this stuff we're doing quiet. We are breaking the law; state and federal. You guys realize that...Right?"

Sonny grinned. "You told us that before. We ain't stupid."

They all had a good laugh as Clint was climbing inside his truck. Clint closed the door and glanced at the three poachers through his rear-view mirror. Then he muttered softly to himself. "Yep, I've warned you twice, and I'm sure the judge will take that into consideration when he decides your fate."

Weeks passed, and Clint hadn't heard anything from Sonny. He was concerned that the investigation was falling apart. It was early September, and the nights were getting colder, good temperatures for poaching deer.

Clint was about to head to the gym for an early morning workout when the phone rang. It was Sonny.

"We got eight deer for you. We need them picked up this afternoon. They're dressed out, skinned, and frozen. If you don't want 'em, we have other customers that do."

"No problem, I'll take them." Clint said.

"Good," said Sonny. "Meet me at the Belch Bar, and then we'll go get them at Bubba's house."

"Okay Sonny, see you in an hour or so."

Sonny was waiting in the parking lot when Clint arrived. Clint motioned for Sonny to get in his truck, and they headed over to Bubba's home while Sonny gave the directions.

Clint was armed, and he was wired with a hidden tape recorder. A state police cruiser and a game commission enforcement vehicle were hidden nearby with two officers in each vehicle. They had been listening while Sonny directed Clint and were ready to respond if things got out of hand.

Bubba's house was a half mile off a blacktop paved road, surrounded by mature trees. Sonny told Clint to back his truck up to the garage door.

Clint was looking in every direction while trying not to appear nervous, but Sonny noticed.

"What's the matter Clint, you scared or something?"

"No, I trust you guys," Clint said sincerely. "I'm just worried about being caught." Clint hoped Sonny believed him.

They were in the middle of nowhere, and if the poachers had suspected he was an agent, there might be trouble when the garage door opened. He didn't know what to expect.

As the garage door slowly rose, Clint zipped his jacket halfway down with his right hand and placed it back on the steering wheel. Now he could easily reach the 9mm Sig Sauer pistol that was tucked into his shoulder holster. Sonny was looking out at the passenger's side mirror and didn't seem to notice.

Clint rolled down his window, giving him a better range of motion with the gun, while praying he wouldn't need to use it.

"Hey there Clint, welcome to my home!" Bubba called as he stepped from the shadows of his garage.

Clint breathed a sigh of relief. "I don't have any scales with me, so we need to estimate the weight again and make up any difference on the next haul. I have scales at the shop."

"No problem, we trust you," Bubba said.

Bubba and Killian lifted the deer carcasses out of a huge chest freezer and loaded them into the capped bed of Clint's pickup. Killian estimated the weight at over eight hundred pounds, and Clint agreed that it was a reasonable guess. He pulled a wad of cash from his jacket pocket, counted out thirteen hundred-dollar bills and placed the money on the open tailgate of his truck. Bubba grabbed it and stuffed the cash into his pants pocket. "Pleasure doing business with you," he said.

Bubba said that they had killed five deer one night and three the next. He said that he had driven while holding the spotlight and Killian shot the deer with a .22 magnum rifle. Bubba and Killian bragged about how quickly they could shoot a deer and load it into their truck. Killian said that he shot each one in the head and claimed that it took no longer than thirty seconds from the time the spotlight went on until the deer was tossed into the back of the truck.

Killian said that he shot one of the deer while it stood in the front yard of someone's house. "You went right past it on the way here, the yellow ranch house just down the road."

"Yep, I know where you mean." Clint said.

Bubba laughed and said that one was still alive in the back of the truck when they got back to his house. He went on to say that he skinned and dressed the deer in the basement of his home, and that he used a sump pump to get rid of the blood after he washed down the floor. He placed the entrails, head, and legs of each deer inside the hide, tied them up and threw them in a ditch several miles away.

"Tell him what you do with the ears," urged Killian.

"Oh yeah," Bubba chuckled. "I cut the right ear off the head of every deer, so the game wardens know it's me when they find the remains. But they don't know who 'me' is." He laughed hysterically.

Killian started laughing so hard he could barely speak. "You forgot about the highway overpass; that one was the best. You gotta tell him about it, man."

"Yep...In the middle of the night, I hung a deer carcass over the bridge where Route 15 crosses Route 220. I used a thick Manila rope with a hangman's noose around its neck. And I attached a cardboard sign painted with big red letters that said, 'Game Warden You're Next.'"

With that remark, everyone broke into a roaring laughter, including Clint. It wasn't easy for him, but he pulled it off. Had to. It sickened him, but he was that rare breed of a man who could immerse himself into the world of the poacher, play the character, and play it well.

Bubba grabbed a large white plastic bag from inside the garage and handed it to Clint. He said that five of the deer Clint purchased were does and three were bucks. The bag held three sets of velvet antlers, and he wanted to know what they were worth. Clint said he would take them to the "boss" to see what they could be sold for in the Asian markets of New York City and get back to him. (*The Chinese have used antler velvet for thousands of years to treat ailments such as high cholesterol, headaches, asthma, indigestion, liver and kidney disorders, ulcers, etc. It is sometimes used in their anti-aging serums to improve blood circulation or to prevent memory loss.*)

Clint was getting weary of all the boasting, so he made up an excuse to get back on the road. He dropped Sonny off at the Belch Bar and headed home.

Later that night, Bubba called. He complained that both he and Killian were unhappy with their working relationship with Sonny and said that they were not going to continue giving him a piece of the action just for making phone calls. Bubba said that he was going to tell Sonny that selling the deer was getting too risky, and that they were going to put an end to it. Then he and Killian would be able to cut him out and keep the money from future kills between the two of them. Bubba asked Clint to call Sonny to back up their lie. Clint said he could make the call but didn't believe it was necessary. "Sonny isn't going to mess with you guys," he said. "If you tell him you're done, he's gonna step aside."

Bubba asked Clint what he would pay for other wild animals, particularly bears. Clint told him he would pay up to $300 for a bear depending on size. "I'm gonna need the entire carcass," explained Clint. "That's what the Asian markets are asking for."

"We'll start working on that in a few days," said Bubba. "Tomorrow, me and Killian are leaving for New York state. We got a suitcase full of marijuana to get rid of. Beer money," he added with a crooked smile."

Clint nodded that he understood.

"We used to run bales of it up to Williamsport from Philadelphia," he said. "Now we get our supply from local folks. Makes life so much easier."

"And more profitable," exclaimed Killian.

Bubba said that he was putting a camper on his truck for the trip to New York and would be bringing back a load of deer and salmon.

"Go for it," said Clint. "I'll buy whatever you can haul back to Pennsylvania."

The following morning, Clint took the eight carcasses—still frozen solid—to a USFWS storage facility with a walk-in freezer and a set of scales. The total weight of the eight deer came to 550 pounds, which was three hundred pounds less than the estimated weight he'd paid for.

Clint telephoned Sonny Day and told him about the problem with the deer and that he had overpaid Bubba and Killian.

"You gotta be real careful with those two," warned Sonny. "Especially Bubba. I don't trust him any farther than I could throw him."

Later that day, Bubba telephoned Clint and said he had talked to Sonny and learned of the discrepancy in the weights. Bubba said that Sonny wanted one-third of the money from the sale of the deer, but that they had not paid him yet. Bubba said it wasn't worth paying him that much to make phone calls and arrange for picking up deer, and that they hadn't decided what his cut would be. Bubba assured Clint they would make up the difference for the weight discrepancy of the eight deer.

A few days later, Killian telephoned Clint and told him that he had killed three deer the previous evening and wanted to get five more later that night.

"I'll take them all," said Clint. "Cash as always."

"How about beef cows?" asked Killian. I know where I can get two. If you want 'em, it'll cost you $300 each at the time of delivery with the balance due after the carcasses are weighed." Killian paused, waiting for Clint to respond, but there was only silence. "I spotted some in a farmer's field," he continued. "I can kill two, gut them and pack the body cavities with ice until you come for them."

Clint couldn't believe what he was hearing. Bad enough they were killing deer and offering to kill bears; there was no way he would allow them to hurt farmers. "If you guys are going to kill livestock for me or anyone else, we are finished. Understood?"

Clint didn't wait for an answer before hanging up.

The following evening, Clint met with Bubba at a bar near the village of Trout Run. During their conversation, Bubba stated he preferred to work alone, and that he didn't like working with Killian because he was a drug addict. He also stated that the partnership with Sonny was over, and that he would make up for the poundage of deer meat he owed because of the weight discrepancy.

Later that evening Clint met with Sonny at the Belch Bar. Sonny said that he was also unhappy with the partnership because he considered Bubba and Killian to be untrustworthy. He stated that he knew others who were killing and selling deer, and he would contact them to arrange for sales to Clint.

The following week Bubba called Clint first thing in the morning. He and Killian had seven deer dressed out, skinned, and in cold storage waiting for him.

"Come and get 'em Clint," he said. "I need to make room in my freezer for more kills."

Clint said he would be at his house by noon. Then he arranged for local game wardens to be standing by in case things got ugly. By now Clint was confident that the poachers didn't suspect he was a federal agent, but he always called for backup as a precaution.

This time Clint brought a hanging spring-scale with him, and each deer was weighed. The total weight came to 550 pounds, so Bubba agreed to deduct three hundred pounds to make up for the overage from the last sale.

"Are we good, now?" Bubba asked.

Clint nodded. "Good as gold."

"Great," said Bubba, "we'll be in touch soon with more deer."

"Listen guys," said Clint, "the boss at Southeast Seafoods told me he is well-stocked with venison. So, like I said from the beginning, we're not asking you to kill deer for us."

"What's that mean?" asked Killian. "You don't want to buy any more deer?"

"What it means is this: We will buy them rather than have you sell to a competitor."

Bubba said, "We'd rather sell to you anyway, Clint. You're easy to deal with, and you pay more than our other customers do."

"That's what I thought," Clint said. "Just wanted to confirm."

Bubba said, "No problem, man. We are dyed-in-the wool poachers. Always have been, always will be. This is how we live. It's our creed…no closed season."

"Understood," said Clint. "Call when you have something for me."

Two weeks later, Bubba called Clint and said he had four deer ready and wanted them picked up as soon as possible. He said he had a six-point buck, two button bucks, and a doe. Bubba said he had a new partner he referred to as "Piker," and that Piker's sister, Debbie would sometimes drive the truck for him and handle the spotlight while he would shoot.

Clint went to Bubba's home the following morning to pick up the deer. Bubba said that he had already paid Piker and his sister for helping to kill them. He bragged that he was keeping track of a large bear that denned up for the winter and planned to kill it in the spring and offer it for sale. The four deer were weighed at two hundred eighty pounds. Clint handed Bubba $420 cash.

A few weeks went by, and Bubba called Clint stating he had eight deer ready for him to pick up. He said that he was still working with Piker, and that Piker had shot most of them while Bubba drove the truck and worked the spotlight. During the conversation, Bubba said that he had some gun silencers that were made by a friend of his at a machine shop in Williamsport. He talked about previous sales of silencers and conversion parts that would modify a semi-automatic rifle to fully automatic. Bubba offered to sell the silencers for $100 each.

Clint arrived at Bubba's house the following morning and weighed the deer for a total of four hundred and ten pounds. He handed Bubba $615 in cash, and after they were loaded into his pickup truck, he took them to the walk-in evidence freezer for storage.

A month passed and Clint hadn't heard from Bubba. Then, unexpectedly, Sonny placed a call to Southeast Seafoods early in the morning. Special Agent Abraham answered the phone.

"Southeast Seafoods, how can I help you?"

"It's Sonny Day. I need to talk to Clint Hammer.

"He is out in the field today sir, but I can have him call you. Do you have some venison ready for us?"

"Yeah, I'll have it real soon. Tell him to call me." And with that, Sonny hung up the phone.

That evening, Clint called Sonny and was told that he had four deer dressed, skinned, and frozen, and that he wanted $150 for each deer.

"That's a lot of money," returned Clint. "They better be big, really big."

"They are." Sonny said. "I'm working with Bubba again. We passed on some smaller deer and shot four big bucks."

Clint told Sonny that he had a client in New York state who was looking for some venison, but there would be some additional risk, as transporting the illegal deer across state lines violated federal laws.

"If you're gonna pay that much, I'll take the risk." He said. "But let's wait a couple days; I think me and Bubba can kill a few more to make the trip worthwhile."

"Works for me," replied Clint. "Call me when you're ready."

Two days later, Sonny called Clint and told him they had ten deer. He said there would be a change of plans, and Bubba would be transporting the deer to New York. "Where do you want him to meet you?" he asked.

"Take Route 14 North across the state line," said Clint. "Go seven miles and you'll see an abandoned warehouse on the right. I'll be waiting in a white Chevy van with the buyer."

Bubba drove his truck loaded with ten deer carcasses and met Clint and Mr. Big (a USFWS Special Agent) at the pre-determined location. Bubba loaded the deer carcasses into the van, and Mr. Big paid him $1500 in cash.

Bubba bragged that he had originally killed enough deer to fill the order, sold half of them to another buyer, and then shot five more to fill the order of ten deer. He said that his wife drove the truck while he shot all of the deer. Each was shot in the head with a .22 magnum rifle. He complained that Sonny was supposed to transport the deer to New York for him, but he couldn't come up with a vehicle, so he had to do it himself. Bubba said he gave Sonny a fifteen percent cut for the sale of the ten deer.

After Bubba left, Clint drove the van to the walk-in evidence freezer and put the deer inside. When he returned home, there as a message from agent Abraham that a man named Spin from Renovo called Southeast Seafoods and said he "had something for Clint Hammer." Agent Abraham said it was time to wrap up the investigation, and that briefings would be conducted the following week involving all of the agents who were actively involved in investigations. A large-scale takedown of the suspects would happen shortly thereafter.

Clint only had a day or two before the mission would end. Time was running out, so he called Spin right after talking with agent Abraham. The phone only rang once.

"Talk to me," said a voice on the other end of the line.

"It's Clint. I was told you have something for me."

"Yeah, I have an eight-point and a ten-point in cold storage. My customers bailed on me, so they're yours if you want them."

"I'll take them both, how much?"

"You know the price; I already told you when we met at Joey's Bar. It's five dollars per point, so we're talking $90 total for both deer."

"No problem Spin. Can I pick them up tomorrow?"

"Yep. Do you want the whole deer or just the heads? I can cut the heads off at the shoulders?"

"I want the entire carcass of each deer."

Clint drove to Renovo first thing in the morning and met Spin at his house at the edge of town. Spin was waiting outside and asked Clint to back his truck up to the garage door.

"Okay, let's get them loaded, I have other stops to make." Clint said.

Spin asked Clint to help him lift the deer out of his chest freezer, and he insisted they cover the carcasses with a tarp before loading them into Clint's truck.

"What are you worried about?" Clint asked.

"With my luck, Wasserman will drive by just as we're loading into your truck. So, I ain't taking no chances."

"Oh yeah, Wasserman the woods cop," Clint remarked. "Sonny mentioned him during one of our buys."

"Yep, that's him."

"You don't have to worry about the state boys," declared Clint. "It's the feds you need to watch out for."

"The feds!" snorted Spin. "That's a laugh. They couldn't find Renovo on a map."

After the deer were loaded, Clint pulled out a wad of cash and peeled off what he owed Spin in ten-dollar bills. "Spin, I gotta run, it was nice doing business with you. I hope to see you again real soon."

"Same here," said Spin. "The sooner the better."

"I'll make a point of it," promised Clint.

As Clint drove away, he couldn't help but smile when he glanced into his sideview mirror and saw Spin wave him off. "Be careful what you wish for" he muttered.

The following week, briefings were conducted in several locations prior to the takedown of suspects from six states and the District of Columbia. In Pennsylvania, team assignments were made during the briefing held at Game Commission headquarters in Harrisburg, which was established as a command center manned by state and federal personnel. Game wardens, including myself, and USFWS agents, were provided instructions for the takedown that would occur within forty-eight hours. We were instructed that the suspects could be told they were the subject of an undercover operation, and the person they were selling wildlife to was an agent of either the USFWS or the Pennsylvania Game Commission as applicable. However, we were to refer to the undercover agents only by their alias names. I was partnered with USFWS agent Williams and assigned to arrest and interrogate Sonny Day.

Two days later, beginning at six o'clock in the morning, state game wardens and federal agents began serving search warrants and arrest warrants. In Pennsylvania alone, eighty-two state game wardens and thirty-three USFWS agents were involved in the state-wide takedown of suspects.

Myself and my deputy 'Ranger' met agent Williams at a pre-determined location near Sonny's home shortly before six o'clock in the morning. We passed the time reviewing protocols, and when the clock struck six, we pulled into Sonny's driveway. It was mid-January, and still dark outside. Ranger was positioned to cover us and stood near our vehicles. He was able to watch the window nearest to the front door of the house.

I rapped on the front door with my fist. "Federal agents!" I shouted. "Open up!"

No response.

I knocked again, louder this time. "Open the door, we have a warrant for your arrest!"

Lights suddenly illuminated the inside of the house.

"He's headed for the door; he's holding a handgun!" Ranger shouted.

I turned toward Ranger. "Quick, hit the red lights."

Ranger jerked opened the door of my patrol truck and switched on my emergency red lights while keeping an eye on Sonny.

"He sees the lights. He's putting the gun down on a table now." Ranger shouted.

We drew our guns as a precaution as the door slowly opened. Sonny immediately placed his hands behind his head; we didn't need to order him to do it. I told him to turn around and place his hands behind his back. Sonny complied.

"What's this all about?" he grunted.

I handcuffed him. "You're under arrest for violating state and federal laws concerning the sale and transportation of deer unlawfully killed. I'm transporting you to the United States Marshall's Service Headquarters in Williamsport where you will be provided with more information."

"I don't know what you're talking about!" wailed Sonny.

I turned him around to face me. "Clint Hammer is an undercover agent for the United States Fish and Wildlife Service. Does his name ring a bell to you?"

Sonny looked down at his feet. "Yes. I guess I'm in a lot of trouble."

"Yes, you are. I'll explain more when we get to the US Marshalls headquarters."

The US Marshall in charge was expecting us when we arrived. I sat down at a table across from Sonny and asked if he was willing to provide a written statement, and that he could be represented by an attorney if he desired. I told him that most of the phone calls between him and Clint Hammer were recorded, and that Clint Hammer was an alias.

"You got me. I'm willing to cooperate if it will help me."

I looked squarely into his eyes. "Sonny...I can't promise you anything, but your cooperation could be considered favorably by the United States Attorney who will be prosecuting this case.

"Okay," he replied. "I'll tell you what I know."

Sonny gave me a lengthy written confession implicating himself, Bubba, Killian, and others in the multiple sales of deer that were unlawfully taken during closed season, and through the use of an artificial light. He pleaded guilty to several state and federal charges, spent some time behind bars, and paid heavy fines. Killian and Bubba suffered similar consequences.

I stopped at Spin's house on my way home. I had a criminal citation to issue to him for the two deer he sold. It was a big fine, hundreds of dollars. He was shoveling snow off the sidewalk when I arrived, so I slowly cruised up to the edge of his driveway and got out of my patrol truck.

"Hi Spin," I said with a broad grin. "Clint Hammer asked me to give you a message."

Spin opened his mouth, but he was speechless for a moment. Then: "I don't know anyone by that name," he said nervously.

I handed him the citation. "Clint said you once told him that the feds couldn't find Renovo on a map. He wanted you to know that despite your firm conviction, he was indeed able to do just that, and he said he'd be happy to return just so he could see your smiling face once again when he testifies against you in court."

During the course of the investigation, undercover agents purchased more than three tons of illegal striped bass, over four hundred ducks and geese, over three hundred deer, as well as bear parts, eagles, hawks, songbirds, rabbits, pheasants, and turkeys. Violations of multiple state and federal wildlife laws, as well as federal narcotics statutes, USDA statutes, explosives statutes, and conspiracy were documented.

One hundred and twenty suspects residing in Pennsylvania, New York, New Jersey, Maryland, Delaware, Virginia, and the District of Columbia were arrested.

Defendants in the investigations were charged under a number of state and federal wildlife laws. Among those was the Lacey Act, a federal law prohibiting interstate commerce of fish or wildlife taken in violation of state law. The maximum penalty for a violation of the Lacey Act was $20,000 and five years of imprisonment.

Most of the fish and wildlife purchased during the investigations were promptly frozen and later distributed to public institutions and charitable organizations.

United States of America vs. Bruno B. Ware

When confronted by federal game wardens, Bruno B. Ware claimed he was an innocent big game hunter and private museum owner who had unknowingly violated federal wildlife laws because they were so confusing and hard to understand.

The United States Fish & Wildlife Service (USFWS) had a different opinion. The agency believed that Mr. Ware deliberately conducted illegal activities involving the importation of endangered species for thirteen consecutive years.

In 1976 Mr. Ware was apprehended by USFWS agents (federal game wardens) while attempting to smuggle the hides of a Nile crocodile and a leopard (both endangered species) into the United States by concealing them inside an elephant hide that was shipped to his museum. While the elephant had been legally taken in Africa, the Nile crocodile and African leopard were prohibited from importation into the United States.

That same year, Ware smuggled another endangered species—a bald eagle—into the United States after having it mounted by a taxidermist in Colorado. A lengthy investigation later revealed that he shot the bald eagle in Canada and brought it into the states by rolling it up inside a mountain lion hide. The big cat had been lawfully killed.

Another incident that deserves mention is when Ware, in 1980, attempted to smuggle the hides and horns of a serow and a goral into the United States via Mexico City. These are antelope-like animals found in Asia. Both species were endangered and required special permits to import them into the United States. After the hides arrived in Mexico, Ware attempted to make connections with a native citizen to recover the hides from Mexican customs in order to evade the legally required American port of entry. Ware directed the Mexican citizen to offer a large sum of cash to a Mexican customs agent in exchange for the hides and horns. Ware backed off his crooked scheme when he learned of the substantial cost and risks involved if he were caught dodging the National Customs Agency of Mexico.

In November 1989, I was asked to assist two USFWS agents in serving a search warrant on Mr. Ware's home and museum. Most federal agents did not wear law enforcement uniforms, and they wanted a uniformed officer on the scene. That is where I fit into the scenario. I had been deputized as a federal agent years earlier, although I was rarely asked to perform any enforcement duties.

One week before the search warrant was to be served, I met with federal agents in Harrisburg, and they briefed me on their probable cause information. Both agents, Leo and Mike, were concerned about Mr. Ware. His reputation was that of a brawler with a bad temper. He was a millionaire with an inclination to use physical force at any time. I was told that Mr. Ware was single, and he lived in his home alone.

His house, a huge mansion, was allegedly brimming with loaded firearms of every description. And there was a saying among the local folks: *Beware of Bruno B. Ware*. Nobody wanted to get this guy upset with them.

It was a chilly November morning when I drove up Mr. Ware's long driveway in my patrol vehicle. The USFWS agents were following close behind me. I couldn't see his house until I rounded a curve a hundred yards away. It was immense. A large, imposing residence built of stone. I crept forward in my truck clearly marked as a Pennsylvania Game Commission vehicle. I made sure the removable red emergency light was attached to the roof, as I wanted to be as conspicuous as possible due to Bruno Ware's reputation as a brawler (red and blue police lights were not used until years later).

I stopped my truck within a few feet of a side entrance to the home, opened my door, and stepped out. A cold breeze embraced me, and I shivered a bit, blaming it on the weather. Truth be known, I wasn't sure what to expect, and my shiver may not have been due to the cold wind alone.

Both federal agents pulled up behind me and guardedly opened each door of their black unmarked sedan. Bruno B. Ware had been arrested by the Feds before, and for all I knew, in his mind, our presence in his driveway might have been enough to take him over the edge. The proverbial last straw that broke the camel's back.

Don't sweat it John, I said to myself, you can overpower this man if it comes to that. After all, I was a champion powerlifter. At six feet and two-hundred-twenty pounds body weight, I was able to deadlift well over six hundred pounds. I was in my prime...but I wasn't bullet proof.

Any time a law enforcement officer knocks on someone's door, it can turn ugly very quickly. Most of the time it doesn't. Problem is...you never know when it may happen, so you always need to be prepared.

I walked up to the door with both agents close behind me and knocked. No response. A dead calm.

Give it a minute, I said to myself. *It's early and perhaps he is sleeping in.*

Once again, a sharp cold breeze brushed my face, and a sense of foreboding crept over me. *Could this be the calm before the proverbial storm?* I thought.

Leo and Mike must have sensed it too, as they cautiously stepped several paces to each side of me, one to my left, and one to my right. They too were armed and ready for whatever may come next.

I pounded on the door with my fist. "United States Fish and Wildlife agents!" I announced. "Open the door; we have a search warrant."

A minute when by, but it seemed like an hour. I was about to knock again when the door slowly opened a few inches, while someone, definitely not Bruno B. Ware, peered at me with only part of his face and a single eye exposed.

"May I ask why you gentlemen are here?" He said nervously.

I pushed my foot against the door. "We have a warrant to search this house, signed by a federal judge. Who are you?"

"I am Mr. Ware's majordomo."

"His butler?" I said surprised.

"My name is Sparrow; I'm his majordomo—his chief of the house. Please do not use such a humiliating description as *butler* to address me."

"Sorry about that. I've never come upon a butler—I mean a majordomo—in this neck of the woods, or anywhere else I've been for that matter."

"Hmmm, perhaps you should travel more."

"Okay, enough with the pleasantries. Open the door or I'll have no choice except to move you aside...Sir."

Sparrow tried to close the door, but my foot prevented it. "First I must call Mr. Ware's attorney," he said as he repeatedly bounced the door off of my size thirteen boot.

"Listen to me Sparrow," I said. "You can call the attorney, but we are coming inside first. So, you need to flutter out of our way...Sir."

Sparrow ignored my comment and continued to push the door against my boot.

"Look at me Mr. Sparrow," I said. "Do you see a badge, a uniform, two other men, and a law enforcement vehicle parked behind me?"

"I, Uhm…"

"No need to answer; it's not a question. We're going inside. If you try to stop us, I'll use force to get past you. My steel-tipped leather boot is lodged against the bottom of the door, and I've run out of patience.

Sparrow lightened his grip on the door. "Force? What kind of force?"

"You don't want to know. Now back off or I'll arrest you for interference with a state officer."

Sparrow stepped back from the door. "You don't have to threaten me, sir!"

"Where is Bruno?" I demanded as we moved inside.

"You mean *Mister* Ware. That is the way he insists we address him."

"Copy that; where is he?"

"Mr. Ware is hunting in Russia, and he won't return until late next week."

Sparrow hurried over to a nearby telephone and started punching buttons with a finger. I walked over and handed him a copy of the search warrant.

"Your attorney will probably want you to read this to him," I said.

Sparrow was thin and short with bleached blonde hair that gathered to form a round bun at the back of his head. He wore a delicate thread of black eyeliner below the lower lashes of his eyes. His eyes were bright green, an improbable color, and likely due to green contact lenses. His ears were pierced with hooped, yellow gold earrings, and he was dressed in a neatly pressed long sleeve white shirt, buttoned at the top and a red and black, plaid Scottish kilt, a type of knee-length men's dress skirt that covers the body from the waist down to the center of the knees. His feet were bare, no socks, no shoes.

The house was immense, and there were mounted specimens everywhere. Many of them were North American species that I was familiar with, and I immediately identified a pied-billed grebe on a coffee table in front of a large couch.

The pied-billed grebe is a small, chunky, swimming bird with a slender neck, and a relatively large blocky head with a short, thick bill. They have virtually no tail. They were considered endangered or threatened in many states, particularly in the northeastern United States, and I doubted that it had been taken legally. The problem with mounted specimens is being able to determine when and where they were killed. Something endangered in the US may not be endangered in Canada, or other countries. And then there was the issue of determining when it was taken. Endangered species taken before the Endangered Species Act was enacted were usually "grandfathered in," meaning the mounts could be legally possessed.

There were other specimens that I couldn't identify, as Mr. Ware hunted all over the world for rare animals. However, the feds had probable cause to believe he was in possession of wildlife specimens that were brought into this country unlawfully.

I looked around the room and noticed a rifle leaning against a sliding glass door behind me. A few feet away from the doorway that we entered was another rifle propped up against the wall. And down a hallway leading to other rooms in the house was still another rifle leaning against a closed door. Each gun was fully loaded. We emptied them and decided it would be best to keep an eye on Sparrow, even though we doubted he knew which end of the gun a bullet came from.

Behind Mr. Ware's desk was a locked door leading to another room. Sparrow was finished talking to the attorney, and I asked him to unlock it.

"I'm sorry Officer Wildman, or whomever you are, but I can't do that."

"It's Wasserman, not Wildman. Only one person calls me wild man, and he's a good friend. Now, are you saying you can't unlock it, or that you won't?"

"I'm not permitted to unlock it sir, it's forbidden by Mr. Ware."

"I don't want to break the lock or damage the door, so give me the key and I'll unlock it myself."

Sparrow smiled, baring gleaming white teeth. He winked in apparent amusement. "Oh, I see, a very sneaky move on your part officer." He eyed me up and down. "You have a dominating way about yourself sir. I will get the key."

Sparrow turned and sashayed across the room to a large desk while I followed close behind him. He opened the top drawer, picked up a key, and spun around to face me. The key was in his right hand, rings on every finger, and he promptly extended his arm straight out and dangled the key between his index finger and thumb.

I held out my hand and he dropped it into my open palm.

"Satisfied?" he asked, batting his eyelashes at me.

"For now," I responded.

I turned and walked over to the locked door, Leo and Mike were staring at me while doing their best not to laugh. I stared back and shook my head from side to side. But I couldn't prevent a wee grin from forming.

I unlocked the door and walked inside with Leo while Mike continued to search the main room while keeping an eye on Sparrow. The first thing I noticed were hundreds of empty twelve-gauge shotgun shells or hulls, packed vertically in their original boxes, with the open end up. Each shotgun shell contained a single tail feather from a grouse. No doubt Bruno B. Ware considered them to be miniature trophies, each one documenting his skill as a marksman. It was his desire to collect trophies, and record his successful hunts, that would come back to haunt him.

While in the room, we seized seventy-five carousel trays containing five thousand photographic slides of his hunting safaris, each one with a notation that included the date of kill for each animal taken. We also seized fifty VHS video tapes, and another large number of eight-millimeter tapes depicting his safaris.

While we were conducting the search of Mr. Ware's home, additional federal agents were at his museum with a rented U-Haul truck. The museum contained mounted specimens of hundreds of animals from all over the world, each one allegedly shot by Mr. Ware. And there were trophy cases full of plane-ticket stubs, expired visas and photographs of Mr. Ware kneeling beside successful kills from his hunting expeditions. The world's largest collection of life-size mounted sheep, and mounted specimens of all twenty-seven species of North American big game recognized by the Safari Club International were inside his museum. Many of the mounted animals were displayed in realistic plastic or synthetic reproductions of their natural habitat. There was a huge Wapiti-Maral stag, similar in appearance to the North American elk that he killed in Outer Mongolia. It was the biggest on record at the time. There was a Sudan Roan, a species of antelope found in Africa that was also the biggest on record. Many of the mounted specimens couldn't be identified by most folks, such as the sitatunga, duiker, bongo, chevrotain, dik-dik, and scores of others.

A large number of mounted specimens at the museum were seized as evidence and loaded into the U-Haul truck. Meanwhile, the search of Mr. Ware's home yielded incriminating documents, notes, photos, slides, and video evidence.

Two months later, Mr. Ware was charged with the importation, receipt, concealment, and transportation of various species of wildlife contrary to the Endangered Species Act, and the Convention on International Trade in Endangered Species (the "CITES" Treaty).

When Congress passed the Endangered Species Act in 1973, it stated that our natural heritage is of "esthetic, ecological, educational, recreational, and scientific value to our Nation and its people." Congress also expressed concern that many of our nation's native plants and animals were threatened with becoming extinct.

The purpose of the Endangered Species Act was and still is to protect and restore imperiled species, and the habitat upon which they depend. It is administered by the USFWS and the National Marine Fisheries Service. The USFWS is responsible for wildlife, while the other is responsible for marine wildlife such as whales and salmon, etc.

Under the Endangered Species Act, plants and animals may be listed as either endangered or threatened. Endangered indicates a species is in danger of extinction throughout all or a most of its range. Threatened indicates a species will probably become endangered within the foreseeable future. Distinct species of plants and animals are eligible for listing as endangered or threatened if they meet specific criteria.

The backbone of CITES is the permit system that oversees international cooperation in conservation and trade monitoring. Permits are issued to individuals, such as Mr. Ware, only if it is determined that hunting and transportation is legal and doesn't threaten the species' survival in the wild. The use of special permits enables wildlife officials to verify that various specimens were legally taken, and that they are legal to transport into the United States.

Certain species of wildlife may not be legally imported back into the United States. For example, it is legal to hunt a cheetah or black-faced impala in Namibia (Africa); however, the United States does not permit the importation of the cheetah or black-faced impala hunting trophies into this country. However, Canada, and many other countries may permit the importation of a cheetah or black-Faced impala trophy into those countries.

So, under certain circumstances, a hunter from the United States may be able to legally hunt and kill a cheetah or black-faced impala, but it would be unlawful to import those animals into the United States. Some countries will allow the killing of threatened or endangered animals for a fee, a very high fee that wealthy hunters can easily afford. So, the Endangered Species Act and CITES helps minimize the taking of these animals, and indirectly helps sustain their populations in their countries of origin. A wealthy big game hunter from the United States has little incentive to kill a rare animal if he or she cannot import that animal back into the United States as a trophy.

Bruno B. Ware was specifically charged with importing, concealing, or bringing into the United States contrary to the Endangered Species Act and CITES the body parts of a serow, a black-faced Impala, an African wild dog (also known as an African painted dog), and the horns of another serow. He was also charged with violating the Endangered Species Act by the possession of body parts of a Jentink's duiker, two gorals, and the antlers of two northern huemuls.

Court Exhibit #1 – Jentink's Duiker

Jentink's duiker *The Book of Antelopes* - Public Domain Photo

The Jentink's duiker stands around thirty inches tall at the shoulder and weigh about one-hundred-fifty pounds, making them the largest species of the duikers. They are gray from the shoulders back, and dark black from the shoulders forward. A white band goes over the shoulders, between the two colors and joining the white undersides. Jentink's duikers have long, thin horns, which curl back a little at the ends, and reach between five and eight inches in length.

Jentink's duikers live mainly in very thick rainforest, where they eat fruit, flowers, leaves, and the stems of seedlings. They are nocturnal, and shelter during the day in dense thickets, usually in pairs. The Jentink's duiker was first recognized as a new species in 1884. The species then vanished until 1948 when a skull was discovered in Liberia.

Court Exhibit #2 - Mainland Serow

Public Domain Photo - *Wikimedia Commons*

The mainland serow is a medium-sized goat-like or antelope-like animal with a mane that runs from the horns to the middle of its back. Only males have horns, and they are light-colored, approximately six inches in length, and curve slightly towards the animal's back. The mainland serow can reach a length of six feet, and up to three feet at the shoulder, with and adults weighing over three hundred pounds.

The mainland serow is found in China, Vietnam, Cambodia, Laos, Myanmar, and Thailand. Its distribution follows forested mountain ranges. The serow prefers steep, rugged hills up to an elevation of fifteen-thousand feet with rocky terrain but can also be found in forests at lower elevations.

Court Exhibit #3 - Black-Faced Impala

Photo credit - *Wikimedia Commons, Yathin Sk*

The black-faced Impala is a subspecies of the common impala native to Angola and Namibia. It is rather easy tell it apart from the common impala, as it is much larger and has a distinct black facial marking. It is also found in different locations than the common impala. Unlike the common impala, the black-faced impala has come close to extinction. There were less than two hundred in the wild when Mr. Ware shot and killed one and unlawfully imported it to the United States.

Court Exhibit #4 - African Wild Dog

The African wild dog is a bulky, solidly built African canine. The species stands twenty-four to thirty inches in shoulder height, measures thirty to forty-five inches in length and has a tail about eighteen inches long. Adults can weigh from forty to eighty pounds. As a wild canine, by mass, only the grey wolf is larger. The African wild dog is lean with noticeably large ears.

African Wild Dog. Photo credit Charles J. Sharp *Wikimedia Commons*

The fur of the African wild dog is much different than other canids, with stiff hairs and no under fur. It is said that African wild dogs can identify each other at distances of up to a hundred yards.

The African wild dog is a very efficient pack hunter of antelopes. They have been known to pursue their quarry at speeds up to forty miles per hour, and to continue the chase for as much as one hour or more in extreme cases. Normally the chase will be brief, perhaps less than two miles, during which the prey animal, if larger in size, will be bitten on the legs, belly, and rump until it stops running. Smaller animals are simply pulled down and ripped to pieces by the pack. Male wild dogs are known to grab warthogs by the nose while other members of the pack attack from the rear and side. Warthogs can be very dangerous, reaching a weight of over three hundred pounds, with two pairs of tusks protruding from the mouth that curve upwards. The lower pair is razor-sharp, and the upper tusks, or canine teeth, can easily reach a length of ten inches.

Court Exhibit #5 - Goral

Goral. Public Domain Photo - *Wikimedia Commons*

The goral is an animal group which is similar to a goat. They are found in India with a goat-like or antelope-like appearance. They are usually found on rocky hillsides at higher elevations.

Gorals usually weigh fifty to ninety pounds, and are about four feet in length, with short, backward-facing horns. Most are light gray in color, but some are dark red-brown with a dark stripe down the spine. They have long hair, which protects them in the cold climates where they are usually found.

Court Exhibit #6 - Northern Huemul

The northern huemul, also known as the taruca, or north Andean deer, is native to South America. The huemul is a medium-sized deer with a heavy body and measures up to five feet in length, with a five-inch tail, and about thirty inches tall at the shoulder. Adults weigh up to one hundred eighty pounds, with adult males much larger than females.

Most of the body is covered with light brown hair and white under the head, neck, and tail. Male adult huemuls have antlers that usually measure only eleven inches in length when fully grown. The antlers consist of only two tines, branching close to the base, and with the rear tine usually larger.

Huemul. Photo credit Chris Fryer - *Wikimedia Commons*

Huemuls are only found in the Andes Mountains in Peru, Bolivia, northern Chile, and Argentina. They usually inhabit elevations of ten-thousand feet, but their preferred habitat in Peru reaches almost 17,000 feet.

Bruno B. Ware was the subject of a four-week-long jury trial where it was alleged that he made many visits to the countries of Africa, Australia, New Zealand, India, Nepal, Iran, Mongolia, Russia, South America, Mexico, Alaska, and several provinces of Canada from 1978 to 1989 in order to shoot trophy class animals for his personal enjoyment, and to display them in his museum.

Mr. Ware's attorney argued that the wording of the law was not clear, and that Ware didn't knowingly violate any laws. He also pointed out that Mr. Ware didn't make any effort to hide the trophies and had them displayed in his museum that was open to the public for a small fee of admission.

The US Attorney who was prosecuting the case claimed that Mr. Ware had over three hundred trophy animals on display, and as a professional hunter, he was aware of what was required by law to import trophy animals into the United States. The unlawful mounted specimens, he exclaimed, were hiding in plain view, and displayed in the museum among hundreds of other animals.

In the end, following the month-long trial, the jury returned guilty verdicts after only three hours of deliberation. Mr. Ware was found guilty of sixteen counts of dealing in parts of animals listed as endangered species, including the importation, receipt, and transportation of wildlife listed on the US Endangered Species Act and protected by CITES.

Mr. Ware was ordered by the court to be held without bail pending his sentencing. The US Attorney noted that Mr. Ware had a number of loaded guns at his house when it was searched. Earlier testimony indicated that an anonymous telephone call was made to the local Pennsylvania State Police barracks, and a female caller said that Mr. Ware would "take out" himself and others if he was sentenced to a jail term.

Three weeks later, Mr. Ware was freed on six-hundred-thousand dollars bail (equal to more than a million dollars in 2022) pending his sentencing after the Federal Judge presiding over the case approved a bail agreement worked out between Ware's attorney, and the US Attorney who was prosecuting the case.

The judge had been very concerned three weeks prior about the number of loaded guns seen in Mr. Ware's home when it was searched. That concern had been eliminated after a daylong bail hearing when an area auctioneer with a federal license to sell, buy and possess firearms testified that upon the request of Mr. Ware's attorney, he removed all of the firearms. A list of forty rifles, and twelve pistols was attached to the bail agreement.

The federal judge performed a pre-sentence investigation before deciding Mr. Ware's fate. A pre-sentence investigation is an investigation into the background of someone after he or she has been found guilty of a crime, and it occurs before the sentencing. Basically, it is an investigation to determine the proper sentence for that crime. Some of the information reviewed during the pre-sentence investigation will include past offenses and police records.

The following were the Court's findings of fact, and conclusions of law in determining Ware's sentencing:

• Ware had asserted to the Safari Club International that the killing and importation of the northern huemuls took place in 1972, before the passage of the Endangered Species Act. If that were true, the huemuls would have been legally possessed. However, Ware had scratched out all of the dates on his slide photographs that showed the hunt of the northern huemuls actually occurred in 1978. The USFWS discovered an obscure manufacturing code located on the back of the Polaroid film used in the slides that verified the film used to record the hunt was manufactured in 1977, proving the animals were taken after the Endangered Species Act became law.

• Ware displayed the Huemul antlers in his museum and entered the antlers in the Safari Club International (SCI) Record Book. The Huemuls were ranked second and eighth in the world. The Huemul which was ranked second in the world was at one time the world record.

• Ware placed the Serow horns on display in the museum. The Serow was ranked twelfth in the world.

• Ware entered the Black-faced Impala in the SCI Record Book. The Black-faced Impala was ranked twelfth in the world. It was proven that a Mr. Williams arranged a safari in Namibia for Ware in 1985 on which Ware hunted and collected the Black-faced impala. Therefore, it was not collected before the Endangered Species Act became law.

• Ware placed the Jentink's Duiker on display in his museum. Ware entered the Jentink's Duiker in the SCI Record Book. The Jentink's Duiker was ranked as number one in the world. The Jentink's Duiker was listed as an endangered species and thus could not be imported into the United States.

• Seized from Ware's residence was a letter from a Doctor Smith stating that the Jentink's Duiker had been donated to Ware by Dr. Smith. The letter was dated March of 1972, nearly seven years before the Jentink's Duiker was listed as an endangered species. This false donation letter was procured by Ware to cover the Jentink's Duiker because Ware had been tipped off about the initiation of a federal investigation into the killing of that animal.

• The bogus letter dated in 1972, was sent to the Internal Revenue Service laboratory for ink analysis. The ink used in the doctor's signature was not manufactured until 1979. Therefore, the doctor's signature could not have been written in 1972. The earliest date would have been some time in 1979 when the Jentink's Duiker was classified as endangered.

• The Jentink's Duiker, a large male, was the number one world record, and, while alive, had significant importance for breeding purposes. Only between one and two hundred Jentink's Duikers existed in the wild.

• The Northern Huemul was listed on both the endangered species and CITES in 1978 and thus was prohibited from importation into the United States. In April 1978 Ware hunted in Peru and killed two Northern Huemuls. Two sets of Huemul antlers were seized from Ware's museum. Mr. Ware falsely claimed the Huemuls were taken in 1972, before the Huemuls were listed as endangered in 1978.

• Photographic slides of the Huemuls were obtained from a slide carousal seized from Ware's residence, and each slide was date-stamped at the time of processing, MAY '78. However, the slide box in which the slides were stored by Ware was (falsely) labeled PERU MOUNTAIN AND JUNGLE HUNT 1972.

• In November 1978 Ware hunted in the country of Nepal accompanied by Dr. Smith. Among the trophies that Ware killed on that trip were two Gorals. The Gorals were listed as both an endangered and CITES species and thus could not be imported into the United States. Ware smuggled them into the country and had them mounted by a taxidermist in Colorado by claiming they were killed before the Endangered Species Act declaration.

• Dr. Smith aided and abetted Ware by producing, at Ware's direction, spurious letters alleging pre-Endangered Species Act donations of the Jentink's Duiker and the Gorals. Dr. Smith's letter purports donation of the Gorals to Ware's museum in 1971, several years before they were listed as endangered.

Bruno B. Ware was sentenced in December of 1990. During the sentencing, the judge said that throughout his twenty-year career, he had never seen a case where guilt was so clearly proven against the defendant.

The judge also said he wanted to know what motivated Mr. Ware to shoot and kill, and then import the protected animals. However, Mr. Ware's attorney said he had no idea. The judge said it was his opinion that Mr. Ware displayed the protected animals because he believed he could "hide them in plain sight" among hundreds of other exhibits.

In arguing for a stiff sentence, the prosecuting attorney asked the judge to consider that Mr. Ware, for more than a decade, exploited endangered species. And that he did so after paying a civil penalty for attempting to smuggle a crocodile skin and leopard hide into the country in 1976.

The judge asked how Mr. Ware could have a commitment to conservation, but then shoot and kill endangered species, including a Jentink's Duiker of which there were less than

153

two hundred in the world? The defense attorney was speechless.

The judge sentenced Mr. Ware to three years in jail and fined him $196,000 (equal to $420,000 in 2022) for importing and possessing endangered species of animals. The trial was the longest of a single individual in the history of the US Fish & Wildlife Service. The federal judge stated that the nine-day presentence conference was the second longest ever held in the United States.

The judge stated that he believed the crimes were not committed without great deliberation and forethought, and probably were directed toward Mr. Ware's goal of having a collection of all major specimens of wildlife presently inhabiting the earth. He also stated that he believed Mr. Ware knew the wildlife involved in the case were protected when he shot them, and that Mr. Ware knew it was unlawful to import them into the United States.

Eight years later almost to the day, on Christmas Eve 1998, Bruno B. Ware was arrested by agents of the U.S. Fish and Wildlife Service at O'Hare International Airport in Chicago. Ware was returning from a hunting trip in China when federal customs and wildlife inspectors found him in possession of two black rhinoceros horns. They also discovered an Argali sheep jawbone, a set of Mongolian gazelle horns, and a Ruger M-77 hunting rifle in his luggage. The black rhinoceros and Argali sheep were protected under the U.S. Endangered Species Act and CITES. The Mongolian gazelle was not protected by U.S. or International laws. However, persons bringing a gazelle, or any wildlife parts (horns, hides, etc.) must declare the items on U.S. Customs documents when returning to the United States. Ware failed to declare any wildlife items to U.S. Customs or Service Wildlife Inspectors.

After being charged for the crimes, Bruno B. Ware pleaded guilty to unlawfully importing endangered wildlife parts, and the unlawful possession of a firearm. Because he was a convicted felon for past wildlife offenses, he could not legally possess a firearm in the United States. Ware was eventually sentenced to ten months in prison with two years supervised probation upon his release and fined ten thousand dollars for violating federal wildlife and firearms laws.

Prosecutors contended that Mr. Ware had taken the rhino horns with him on a hunting trip to China in hopes of selling them but was unsuccessful and returned to the U.S. with the horns. In China, the horns are ground up and used to treat fevers, strokes, and comas.

In 1998 when Ware was arrested at O'Hare International Airport, black rhino numbers had declined worldwide by a whopping ninety-eight percent to less than twenty-five hundred animals, an historic low. Since then, the species has made an extraordinary comeback from the brink of extinction. Because of conservation efforts throughout Africa, black rhino numbers have nearly doubled to more than five thousand today. Around the year 1900 it is estimated that several hundred thousand lived in Africa.

Black Rhino photographed by the author

The black rhino species overall is considered critically endangered, with three of the five subspecies having been declared extinct. Poaching and the underground trafficking of rhino horns still threaten its recovery today. Black rhino horns sell by kilograms in weight, with the average horn valued at about one hundred thousand dollars.

On Christmas Eve 2002, Bruno B. Ware took a walk in the woods behind his house. After traveling a short distance, he sat down on a moss-covered tree stump, placed the muzzle of his favorite .45 caliber Colt 1911 against his right temple, and pulled the trigger. There was no note.

He was buried on his estate with a modest tombstone inscribed only with his name, date of birth, and date of death.

No one will ever know why Bruno B. Ware took his own life on that Christmas Eve, the fourth anniversary of the day he was apprehended at O'Hare International Airport in Chicago.

However, he did leave a last will and testament, with everything he owned awarded to his majordomo, Sparrow. It is said that the first thing Sparrow did after the reading of the will, was to remove every remaining mounted specimen from the house. Sparrow hired a backhoe to excavate a large ditch beside Bruno B. Ware's grave, and all of the mounts were dumped inside, covered, and seeded with the finest Kentucky bluegrass he could buy.

"Dust magnets." He said when asked about the trophies. "And some of my guests were frightened of them!"

Choo-Choo

Back in 1950, the Twain family settled in a rustic log cabin along the banks of the West Branch of the Susquehanna River. The cabin had been constructed in Clinton County more than a century earlier on a narrow strip of land between the river and the railroad. Vibrations created by the steady rumble of freight trains—often consisting of more than a hundred cars—shook the cabin so much that all of the family pictures hung crookedly on the interior walls. The chinking between the well-seasoned logs was cracked and crumbling, and a variety of tree seedlings sprouted nearly two feet tall from the sod-covered roof.

The Twain's first and only child, a boy, was born in that cabin on a brutally cold February evening. He was exceptionally large, weighing over thirteen pounds at birth. During the pregnancy, his parents discussed charming potential nicknames for their first child, but those discussions often ended in an argument. They just couldn't see eye to eye on the subject. However, when the big day finally arrived, the time had come for an agreement. Mr. Twain was sitting beside the bed while his wife held their newly born child. Suddenly the cabin began to vibrate softly as a freight train approached in the distance. Mrs. Twain's teacup quivered against its saucer, and soon the locomotive's huge, forged-steel wheels made a thunderous *clickety-clack* against the neighboring track rails. The train blew a long, earsplitting blast from its air-horn as it passed the cabin and slowly made its way south. That's when Mr. Twain got a gleam in his eye, pulled his corn cob pipe from his mouth, and smiled a gummy toothless grin.

"Choo-Choo," he exclaimed. "Let's call him Choo-Choo!"

Mrs. Twain smiled back at him. "Perfect," she said.

Baby Choo-Choo would someday become one of the most notorious poachers in Clinton County, and one of my greatest challenges as a state game warden. It wasn't that he was so smart…he was just very lucky.

By the time Choo-Choo became an adult, he stood six-foot-six and weighed three hundred fifty pounds. Dirty blond hair (more dirt than blond) brushed his shoulders, and a scruffy full beard sprouted from his typically expressionless face. His vacant, deep-set eyes and thick protruding forehead portrayed a menacing appearance. He reminded me of "Bluto," the bearded, muscular bully who was the arch enemy of "Popeye the Sailor Man," a popular cartoon series dating back to when I was a child. Popeye could only defeat Bluto after he swallowed an entire can of spinach (which he would do in a single gulp). The spinach miraculously provided him with a superior strength-boosting capacity.

Choo-Choo didn't have many friends. I'd often see him with his wife, and that was usually while the two of them were road-hunting. They were always cruising the forestry roads, and never seemed to have any success. At least that's what they wanted me to think. Choo-Choo was an excellent marksman and could easily drop a deer with a single well-placed shot. If it was cold enough, he would leave the scene immediately, only to return after dark for the carcass. Sometimes he would first dress out the deer, then cover it with brush and leaves. He wouldn't risk transporting it during the day, even in the open season, since the deer would never be tagged as required by law. This method put the odds in his favor, as he didn't believe in hunting seasons or bag limits.

"Ramming" was another method that Choo-Choo used to poach deer. He had a metal grid made out of steel reinforcing rods (rebar) welded to the front of his truck, and he regularly cruised the roadways looking for what he called "opportunities." The rumor was that he could eat the entire front shoulder of a deer in one sitting. Choo-Choo was always hungry, always looking for "opportunities".

In his early days, Choo-Choo worked part-time at an automobile repair garage near Lock Haven along with a good friend of mine named Jack.

Each year in early spring, I would bring my culvert bear trap to the garage for routine service after having stored it over the winter. The trap was essentially a four-foot-wide steel culvert mounted on wheels with a sliding trapdoor on one end. When a bear enters the culvert and pulls on the bait, the entrance door slams down, preventing the bear from escaping.

On one occasion, after Jack finished lubricating and rewiring the trap, he hauled it outside to the parking lot, opened the door and set the trigger. Then Jack asked Choo-Choo to crawl inside and test the trigger. There were a few dried bear droppings scattered on the floor of the trap from the prior season, and I understand it took quite a bit of coaxing to convince Choo-Choo to crawl inside. He eventually consented.

When he pulled the trigger, the solid steel trapdoor slammed shut with a resounding clang, and Choo-Choo, realizing that he had been tricked, hurled a string of profanities at his captor. But Jack wasn't listening. Whenever a customer would stop at the garage, curiosity would compel them to go have a peek at Choo-Choo inside the trap.

When I stopped by to pick up the trap that afternoon, Jack was nowhere to be found. Some kindhearted soul had released Choo-Choo, and I was told that Jack had wisely decided to leave for home early that day. However, Jack was already planning another hoax, and I would be his unwitting accomplice.

One afternoon, I brought my state patrol vehicle to the garage to have a toggle switch installed; this was just what Jack had been waiting for. He concealed a walkie-talkie radio inside the glove compartment, close to the speaker for my two-way radio. Then he waited for Choo-Choo to climb into the car and begin installation of the switch. As soon as he was inside my vehicle, Jack hustled to the other end of the garage and hid behind a large standing tool chest. He had another walkie-talkie hidden under some boxes near his hideout. Jack disguised his voice and began whispering into the walkie-talkie, pretending he was a Game Commission radio dispatcher.

Choo-Choo stopped what he was doing. A mischievous grin spread across his face as he listened to what he thought was a confidential message being transmitted on my Game Commission radio. The garage was as silent as a tomb.

Suddenly the tranquility was shattered! Choo-Choo bellowed something about game wardens that were headed toward his house and bolted out of my car like a man possessed. He raced out of the building and jumped into his pickup truck, spinning wheels as he raced off the lot toward his home.

Choo-Choo had the gas pedal floored, and he was way over the speed limit for the city of Lock Haven when a police cruiser gave chase, but the officer was forced to back off due to an incoming emergency call.

Rumor has it that Choo-Choo believed the police car never caught up to him because he was going so fast that his truck was just a blur.

Jack never told me exactly what he said over the walkie-talkie, but I understand it had something to do with a search warrant that was about to be served on Choo-Choo's home. Again, rumor has it that a lot of venison ended up in the river that afternoon.

Jack was a good friend of mine, and a great practical joker who unfortunately met with a tragic end years later when he was accidently electrocuted while repairing a Conrail train car. May he rest in peace.

Over the years, there were several incidents where I came very close to nabbing Choo-Choo, but luck always seemed to be on his side. One of those incidents happened in the big woods near Renovo many years ago. Just to clarify, the "big woods" near Renovo consisted of 1.5 million acres of state forest land.

Donnie P was hunting on a grassy pipeline near the headwaters of Shintown Run, a remote, pristine brook trout stream deep inside Sproul state forest. Ten years earlier, I caught him and his father while they were jacklighting deer near Kettle Creek. His father, a plumber by trade, was known as the "Punxsutawney Poacher." At the time, Donnie P was just a young lad who was about to turn eighteen. I charged his dad with some serious Game Law violations, but I let Donnie off the hook after a stern warning and a lecture about fair chase. Donnie promised me he would never poach any wild animal again, and I believed him.

Years later, Donnie was out hunting when he spotted a fawn deer grazing on the grassy pipeline below his position. It was buck season, antlered deer only, and this little deer was safe from Donnie's gun.

While watching the deer, Donnie could hear a motor vehicle slow down and stop below his position, just out of his sight.

Moments later, a shot was fired from below him and the fawn jumped straight up in the air then bolted into the woods. Donnie was certain the fawn had been hit. Next a man carrying a rifle appeared and began walking up the pipeline. He was about six feet tall, wearing blue jeans and an orange hunting coat. Suddenly an adult doe stepped out from behind a cluster of white pine trees on the edge of the pipeline.

The hunter signaled with his hand to someone on the roadway and then immediately took aim at the doe and fired a single shot. The doe stumbled and dropped to the ground.

Grassy pipeline near the headwaters of Shintown Run.

As Donnie started down the pipeline toward the road to confront the hunter, he watched him drag the illegally killed doe into the woods and out of sight.

When Donnie stepped onto the road, he saw a very large man standing near a brown Ford Bronco. Donnie decided it would be best to walk away, but not before memorizing the license plate number. Later that evening, Donnie called me on the phone.

"John, this is Donnie P. I'll never forget the break you gave me years ago. I owe you for that. I saw something you need to know about."

Donnie was just a teenager the last time we talked, and I never expected to hear from him again. Many years had passed since that day. He explained everything to me and described the man standing near the Bronco as "a very large scary looking guy with a heavy beard and long dirty blonde hair."

We made arrangements to meet at the pipeline the next morning, and I found blood and deer hair at the spot where Donnie witnessed the doe being shot. I gathered some blood-soaked leaves and a small piece of muscle tissue as evidence, and then we followed a trail of blood and hair leading to the roadway. The deer had been dragged through the woods in a grueling route over fallen logs, rocks and other obstacles instead of directly down the grassy pipeline. The suspect wanted to be sure no one saw him as he brought his closed season kill back to the road.

I thanked Donnie for the help, we shook hands and parted ways, but not before he volunteered to testify in court if I needed him.

I ran the license plate from the Bronco, and it was registered to Earl "Early" Burd, a local poacher I had been chasing for many years without success.

I was able to get a search warrant for Early's house, and my deputy Ranger and I served it that evening. We found a quartered deer carcass that was partially frozen in a chest freezer, and the heart of a deer in the refrigerator.

Early admitted that he was hunting at the pipeline earlier in the day and claimed that he didn't have any luck.

"My witness tells a different story," I said.

Early chuckled. "Then your witness is a great storyteller."

"Who were you hunting with?" I asked.

"I was with Choo-Choo, and he's gonna tell you the same thing."

Early said that Choo-Choo stayed near his truck while he walked up the pipeline, saw a six-point buck, shot at it and missed. He claimed the venison in his freezer, and the heart, were from a seven-point buck his brother killed two days earlier. He took us out behind his home and showed us the severed head with his brother's kill tag attached to the antlers.

In my opinion, there was no way the deer in his freezer had been there for two days. So, we seized it for evidence and gave him an official receipt. I told Early that I was going to have some lab work done on the venison. If it was a doe, he would be charged with a closed season kill. If it was a buck, I'd return the venison to him, adding that it would be well preserved in our evidence freezer.

From there, we went directly to Choo-Choo's home. As I approached the front door, Choo-Choo pulled up the driveway in his pickup truck. He swung out of the truck and came toward us with his hands closed into tight fists, clearly aggravated by our presence. He admitted being with Early at Shintown Run and said Early shot at and missed a spike buck.

"Early told me he shot at a six-point buck," I said. "Now you're telling me it was a spike. I don't believe either one of you."

Choo-Choo shrugged coolly. "That's all I have to say about it. Now get off my property unless you're gonna arrest me."

I was convinced Choo-Choo had helped Early drag the doe and load it into the Bronco. Assisting to transport an unlawfully killed deer was a serious Game Law violation, but I had no proof. Unfortunately, we had no choice at the time other than to leave his property as he demanded.

The following day, I cut off a small sliver of venison from Early's deer and sent it to the US Fish & Wildlife Forensics Lab in Oregon for analysis. A few weeks later, I received a lab report in the mail confirming that the sample I sent was from a female white-tailed deer.

Later that day, I confronted Early with the lab report, and he admitted that the deer he killed was a doe. "Okay, you got me," he said. "But Choo-Choo didn't have anything to do with it."

"That's hard for me to believe." I replied.

"Like I said, it's all on me. Even if Choo-Choo helped me, I'd never admit it. I don't rat on my friends."

I filed charges against him for killing a doe in closed season and Early pleaded guilty, paid a heavy fine, and had his hunting and trapping privileges revoked for three years.

A year passed, and I was getting a lot of complaints about illegal road-hunting during the archery season in advance of the upcoming rifle deer season. Most of the complaints originated from folks who lived near a state forest road in close proximity to the village of North Bend (the Game Law required hunters to be at least twenty-five yards from the road after alighting from a motor vehicle before shooting at wildlife).

This was a situation that begged for a deer decoy operation, and I had the perfect spot in mind. I contacted my neighboring officer, State Game Warden Ken Packard, and we set up early in the morning of the second day of deer season. Our decoy was a mounted six-point buck lying down with its head and neck erect. The internal motor used to rotate the head from side to side had been disabled by a rifle shot the year before, but the mount was so realistic that I didn't think it would matter.

We placed the deer beneath a hemlock tree about forty yards from the roadway and partially concealed it with brush. We arranged it in such a manner that most people driving by wouldn't see it, while those who were road-hunting had a reasonably good chance of spotting it. It was a small six-point, not a trophy rack by any stretch, and it certainly wouldn't entice anyone to target it who wasn't already predisposed to shooting from the road.

Ken was dressed in camouflage and concealed in heavy brush away from the line of fire. He was using a video camera to record anyone shooting at the decoy. Ranger was positioned in a Game Commission patrol car hidden nearby, and I was stationed out of view just up the road where I could write citations or pursue anyone fleeing the scene. Ranger was assigned to escort violators to my position, and then return to the decoy operation.

Almost immediately, we had our first shooter, and it didn't take long before violators were lined up near my patrol car waiting for their turn to be handed the appropriate citations. Within two hours we apprehended sixteen people, and sadly, all of this road hunting was occurring on the morning of the second day of a two-week-long deer season. Most of the violators never intended to go into the woods on foot and hunt. They were satisfied to shoot out of their vehicles, or to step out and shoot from the road.

The oldest violator that day, Teddy Bare, was ninety-four years old! Teddy had been chauffeured by his eighty-five-year-old friend Sleepy Smith, and he was sitting in the back seat of Sleepy's Chevy sedan when he shot at the decoy.

When Ranger escorted their vehicle to me, Teddy climbed out of the back seat and shambled toward me wearing tawny bedroom slippers fashioned with little rabbit ears, two red eyes, and a white cottontail. I wasn't sure if his unstable gait was due to the loose-fitting slippers, his age, or both. Teddy asked if I was going to arrest him, his eyes wide under thick glasses, his face lined with worry.

"How about we get you back in your car and I'll explain everything," I said in a reassuring manner.

I walked close beside him, ready to grab his arm if he stumbled, and opened the back door of the sedan. As I began to help him back inside, Sleepy started driving off while Teddy only had one leg in the car.

"Stop!" I shouted, yanking Teddy back from the open door.

Fortunately, the car came to an abrupt halt, and Teddy wasn't harmed. At this point, my main concern was getting them safely on their way home. I told them they would receive written warnings in the mail, not a fine, and it had an immediate calming effect on the two elderly men.

"I'm going to include a permit application for you to legally hunt from a parked vehicle," I told Teddy. "There are certain disability requirements and rules you need to meet, but I think your permit will be approved."

Teddy smiled and extended his right arm toward me for a handshake. "Thank you, sir. I heard you were a tough guy, but you ain't. You have a tender heart."

"You better get out of here before I change my mind," I said with an easy grin.

Soon after Teddy and Sleepy drove away, Ranger escorted another violator to my position.

It was Choo-Choo Twain!

After trying for years, we finally caught him. And it was a rock-solid case captured on video. Choo-Choo shot at the decoy while seated in his truck, never even bothering to open the door and step outside.

Choo-Choo was his usual arrogant, cocky self, so I didn't have anything to say to him. *Why waste my time*, I thought. Ranger stood by while I wrote two citations and handed them to Choo-Choo. He said nothing as he snatched the papers from me; he just stared back with hatred in his eyes.

During my long career as a state game warden, there were two poachers who I believed would have shot me in the back if they knew they would get away with it. Choo-Choo Twain was one of them. Vito "The Blade" was the other (from my book *Woods Cop: Thirty-Four Years a State Game Warden*).

Over the years, everyone I had ever cited for shooting at a decoy deer pleaded guilty. After all, the whole thing was captured on video. Many of them would simply ask if they could look at where their bullet struck the decoy as a kind of twisted memento of the day.

Choo-Choo was the first and only suspect in my career that pled not-guilty and took the case to court. And he hired the best attorney in Clinton County, Charles "Stormy" Knight, to defend him.

Stormy Knight never lost a Game Law case in the courtroom. I don't think he ever lost a case of any kind, no matter who he represented or what the circumstances were.

But Game Law violations were his specialty, and I knew it was going to be very difficult for me to get a conviction.

Stormy was an avid hunter who travelled all over the world in big game safaris. He also spent a lot of time hunting the big woods of Clinton County, and he knew the Game Law like the back of his hand.

When Choo-Choo's big day in court finally arrived, he strolled into the courtroom with a defiant smile and Stormy Knight by his side.

I believed my evidence was strong, but I was concerned that Stormy would find a weak link somewhere. This is where he shined. He was a master of persuasion, an eloquent speaker, and he always prevailed. If anyone could convince a judge that Choo-Choo wasn't guilty, it was Stormy Knight.

What's unusual here is that Stormy and I were friends. I knew him since he was in law school, and I was close to some members of his family. Nevertheless, we could go head-to-head in the courtroom, fight to the finish, leave no stone unturned, and still shake hands when it was over. Choo-Choo knew this, just as he knew Stormy Knight was his only chance of getting a not guilty verdict.

While Game Warden Packard testified before the judge, Choo-Choo was whispering in Stormy's ear and shaking his head side-to-side. It was obvious he was disagreeing with Packard's account of what happened, and mumbling lies to Stormy about the incident.

I was seated at the prosecutor's table on the other side of the room and couldn't help but smile. I never told Choo-Choo that we had a video recording of him shooting at the decoy. When I turned on the TV monitor and played the video of him firing a rifle from inside his truck, his mood changed, and the whispering stopped.

After presenting all of my evidence to the court, it was time for Stormy Knight to earn his pay. That meant Stormy had to present a defense, and he was well prepared to do so. He claimed we used *entrapment* (a legal term) to encourage or entice Choo-Choo into shooting at the decoy deer. Stormy argued that had we not presented the opportunity, by way of a decoy deer, Choo-Choo wouldn't have taken the shot. As I expected, he asked the court to dismiss my case because I unlawfully entrapped his client.

However, there is a legal definition for entrapment, and in my opinion the circumstances surrounding this case did not fit. I argued that there wasn't any *encouragement* from game wardens for Choo-Choo to shoot at the decoy, a key element of entrapment under the law. We merely provided an opportunity—the decoy deer—for someone already inclined or willing to shoot from the road.

I compared our decoy operation to when the police park a fancy car as a decoy in a high crime area where vehicle theft is a problem and lie in wait for someone to steal it. And I introduced favorable appellate court decisions accepting the use of decoys by law enforcement in various other situations.

The judge agreed with my argument and refused to dismiss the case. At this point, Stormy's only remaining option was to put his client on the witness stand. That meant Stormy really didn't have any options. No attorney in his right mind would allow Choo-Choo to open his mouth on the witness stand.

The judge found Choo-Choo guilty and imposed the maximum penalty. The fines and attorney fees amounted to a large sum of money, and I was delighted with the court's ruling.

Choo-Choo's anger was undisguised. His jaw was tightly clenched, and his hands formed into huge fists as he glared at me in contempt before storming out of the judge's office. Akin to a freight train, the huge man barged through the exit door with such force that it nearly snapped off its hinges.

The following year, State Game Warden Ken Packard and I teamed up for another decoy operation. Once again it was during the deer season, and we used the same decoy, even though it was nearing the end of its life expectancy. This time we placed it adjacent to a remote unpaved state forest road in Leidy Township, near Kettle Creek. Within minutes after setting it up, a pickup truck approached. Ken was safely hidden in camouflage clothing where he could watch the decoy, and I was positioned close by in my patrol vehicle.

The truck stopped directly across from the decoy, and within seconds a rifle barrel protruded from the passenger side.

BOOM! The crack from the gunshot echoed throughout the hollow. Both occupants of the truck were stunned when Ken suddenly materialized from the thick brush with badge in hand.

"Halt! State game warden," he commanded.

I arrived on the scene within seconds and escorted the shaken hunters away so the decoy would become operational again.

When I checked the shooter's hunting license, I found that the antlered deer tag was detached, and he admitted placing it on an eight-point buck that he killed earlier in the day. The season limit was for a single antlered deer, so I issued citations for both violations.

As the day continued, several vehicles passed by the decoy without taking notice. As evening approached, we decided to wrap it up. Ken was about to remove the decoy when he heard a vehicle coming a short distance away. I watched closely as the approaching truck slowed down and stopped adjacent to the decoy. Suddenly the driver began blasting the horn inside his truck.

I could hear two men in the truck shouting something, but I couldn't understand what they were saying. After a moment, I realized that the truck belonged to Choo-Choo Twain. He and another man were screaming obscenities at the top of their lungs. Choo-Choo recognized the decoy, and their synchronous obscene name calling was directed at me and any other game wardens that may have been hidden nearby. I radioed to Ken and suggested we give them a minute, and they would probably move on.

"Let Choo-Choo and his buddy blow off some steam," I said.

"Okay John," Ken responded. "It's too bad that Choo-Choo knows it's a decoy, because his passenger is holding a rifle and he started to point the barrel out the window."

The screaming ended abruptly, and as Choo-Choo pulled away he turned his head, craned his neck, and spotted my partially concealed vehicle on a hill overlooking the decoy. He shouted one final obscene insult at me as he continued driving away. I can take a certain amount of guff, but Choo-Choo brought me close to my limit of tolerance.

Suddenly, Ken radioed that a black Ford truck was approaching the decoy. It was coming from the south, just as Choo-Choo had done. I watched as the truck slowed to a crawl, finally stopping directly across from the decoy, about a hundred yards behind Choo-Choo.

Then, unexpectedly, Choo-Choo's truck taillights flashed bright red as he hit the brakes.

What's he up to now? I thought.

The passenger in the Ford truck eased open the door and slid out with a rifle.

Choo-Choo and his passenger stumbled out of their truck as the hunter slowly raised the rifle to his shoulder.

"DON'T SHOOT, IT'S A DECOY!" they shouted frantically.

Hearing this, the hunter jerked his gun barrel toward the sky and jumped back into his truck.

My blood pressure soared like a rocket as I struggled to control my feelings. Crazy as it seems, I thought of Popeye (the sailor man) and his famous declaration when he reached a tipping point: *"That's all I can stands; I can't stands no more!"* I actually muttered it under my breath, but unlike Popeye, I didn't whip out a can of spinach, down it in one gulp, and flex my muscles before putting a whupping on my adversary. *Where's a can of spinach when you need it?*

Instead, I grabbed the microphone off my mobile radio and keyed the switch. "Okay Ken," I said, "let's scoop them up!"

I drove downhill to Choo-Choo's truck as Ken jogged over to our position. The passenger was standing on the opposite side of the truck, partially out of view. Choo-Choo stood his ground, an open can of beer in his hand. Then, as I exited my truck, the passenger walked into view.

It was Early Burd. He too was holding a can of beer with a big dopey grin on his face. He raised the can to his mouth, took a sip, and burst out laughing. Choo-Choo did the exact same thing. Ken looked at me, clearly bewildered by their behavior.

"Okay, what's so funny?" I said to them.

Choo-Choo clenched his hand tight, crushing his can of beer, and tossed it into the woods. "I guess we just don't like game wardens," he chuckled merrily.

"Dumb and dumber," I mumbled, barely loud enough for Ken to hear me. They weren't drunk, but they had consumed enough booze to erase any hint of common sense.

"You two can keep on laughing while I write your collection of citations," I told them.

"What for?" Choo-Choo scoffed. "We weren't dumb enough to shoot at your stupid decoy."

"For starters, I'm charging both of you with obstructing a law enforcement operation, and disorderly conduct," I said. "Those offenses are much more serious than shooting at a decoy."

Choo-Choo and Early stopped laughing.

Because Ken saw Early holding a rifle earlier, I also charged him with hunting while on revocation. He was only six months away from having his hunting privileges reinstated; this would set him back for another three years.

Choo-Choo and Early stood silently as they watched Ken and I write out their citations. When we finished, we handed the paperwork to them and sent them on their way.

We were about to head home when a twinkle of light glanced off an object under a stand of laurels.

"Choo-Choo's beer can," I grumbled. I walked over and picked it up.

Ken smiled. "Let's be nice, John," he said sarcastically.

"Okay," I replied. "I won't chase them down to hand out another citation. I'll be nice instead and send it in the mail."

A few weeks later, Choo-Choo and Early pleaded guilty to all of the citations I filed against them, paid heavy fines, and had their hunting and trapping privileges revoked for many years.

Epilogue

Doctor Killem arrived at Albany General Hospital much earlier than he normally would have on this cold mid-winter morning in upstate New York. Nurse April Schowers had scheduled too many surgeries for the day, and he planned to speak with her about it later. This wasn't the first time, and it had to stop.

Doctor Killem was close to retirement, and he hated days like this. By the time he wrapped up all of the operations and drove home, he'd be too tired for anything but a good night's sleep.

He liked April. She was a good nurse in every respect except scheduling. He knew it was because she cared so much for the sick and elderly who relied on the hospital to make them well. The patients and their families loved her. Each year, during the month of May, her office would be flooded with flowers of every description as a reminder of their gratitude for her kindness and dedication.

Doctor Killem chuckled sourly as he slid out of his Mercedes Benz and walked toward the front entrance of the hospital. April was on his mind. *"April Schowers bring May flowers,"* her patients would sing when they dropped them off. *They thought it was funny...but when you've heard it a thousand times the humor tends to wear thin. Even so, April smiles and laughs like it's the first time in her life she's ever heard anyone say it. What a trooper*, he thought. *No wonder everyone loves her.*

Trooper or not, however, he had to tell her to stop scheduling so many surgeries on the same day. And he cringed when he thought how she'd take it. *She's gonna look up at me with those big brown eyes and then she's gonna cry. I just know it!*

Doctor Killem stepped through the revolving front door of the hospital and walked inside, still deep in thought. He was a healer, a fixer; perhaps the best surgeon in upstate New York, and scolding a good nurse was against his creed.

April Schowers saw him in the hallway as he started toward his office and hurried over. "He's responsive!" she cheered.

"Who?" the doctor grunted.

"The man in room ten."

"John Doe, you mean! The patient who's been in a coma for two years?"

"Yes, yes. Isn't it wonderful? He hasn't said a word yet, but he's been howling like a wolf for the last two hours. I think he's having nightmares. I hope he opens his eyes and says something soon."

"Okay, let's go have a look, I don't have time for werewolf stories."

Doctor Killem and Nurse Schowers were about to enter room ten when a patient seated in a wheelchair in the hallway stopped them. "Hey Doc, I can't believe that guy finally woke up."

"Well, I guess howling like a wolf is better than nothing." The doctor grumbled.

"That ain't no wolf," The patient replied. I've been hunting and trapping coyotes all my life, and that there is the perfect imitation of a mated pair of coyotes. He's got the male howling while the female introduces her yips, barks, and howls down perfectly. It's inhuman what this guy is doing. I've never heard anything like it outside of the wild."

When Doctor Killem and nurse Schowers stepped inside room ten, the patient was unresponsive. Doctor Killem checked his vital signs, and everything was normal. "Refresh my memory, April," he said. "Where did this guy come from?"

"All we know is that someone removed him from the bed of a pickup truck late at night, carried him to the emergency room door, rang the bell, and disappeared".

"That's it?"

"Yep. The nurse on duty said some huge bear-like man came to the door carrying him across his arms like a baby before he set him down and disappeared. It was too dark to get a good look at the man."

Doctor Killem shook his head, clearly annoyed. "Wolf men, bear men, good grief! I need a vacation. We need to do a complete neurological exam first thing tomorrow, nurse. But right now, I need your assistance with surgeries. Let's go."

"Yes, doctor, I'll be right with you," she said as she scurried toward a single window. "I just want to open the curtains, so Mr. Doe gets some sunshine. Maybe that will make him feel better."

Doctor Killem rubbed his forehead wearily. "Okay, just be quick about it," he said, storming out of the room into the hallway.

April pulled a nylon cord that dangled by the curtains, opening them as far as they'd go. "I hope this makes you feel better," she said, never expecting a reply.

The man in the bed slowly opened his eyes and stared at the ceiling. "Lovely," he whispered.

April rushed out of the room and ran down the hallway. "Doctor Killem," she shouted, "the coyote man is waking up!"

John Wasserman, a former Pennsylvania Police Olympics champion powerlifter, has written two books about his life as a state game warden. Wasserman retired from the Pennsylvania Game Commission after thirty-four years of service. He lives in the big woods of northcentral Pennsylvania with his wife Denise Mitcheltree, who served as a Pennsylvania state game warden for twenty-two years. He is a professional photographer whose images have been published worldwide.

WOODS COP

Thirty-four Years
A State Game Warden

JOHN WASSERMAN

11·18·22 WOR